A gift for:

_____

From:

_____

Live Loved

EXPERIENCING GOD'S PRESENCE
in EVERYDAY LIFE

MAX LUCADO

COUNTRYMAN ®

A Division of Thomas Nelson Publishers
Since 1798
www.thomasnelson.com

Live Loved

© 2011 by Max Lucado

Published in Nashville, Tennessee, by Thomas Nelson. Thomas Nelson is a registered trademark of Thomas Nelson, Inc.

Thomas Nelson, Inc. titles may be purchased in bulk for educational, business, fund-raising, or sales promotional use. For information, please e-mail SpecialMarkets@ThomasNelson.com.

Unless otherwise noted, Scripture quotations are taken from The New King James Version®. © 1982 by Thomas Nelson, Inc. Used by permission. All rights reserved.

Scripture quotations marked KJV are from the King James Version. Scripture quotations marked MSG are from *The Message* by Eugene H. Peterson. © 1993, 1994, 1995, 1996, 2000. Used by permission of NavPress Publishing Group. All rights reserved. Scripture quotations marked NCV are from the New Century Version®. © 2005 by Thomas Nelson, Inc. Used by permission. All rights reserved. Scripture quotations marked NLT are from the Holy Bible, New Living Translation. © 1996, 2004. Used by permission of Tyndale House Publishers, Inc., Wheaton, Illinois 60189. All rights reserved. Scripture quotations marked God's Word are taken from God's Word, a copyrighted work of God's Word to the Nations Bible Society. Quotations are used by permission. Copyright © 1995 by God's Word to the Nations Bible Society. All rights reserved. Scripture quotations marked JB are taken from The Jerusalem Bible. Copyright © 1966, 1967 and 1968 by Darton, Longman & Todd Ltd. and Doubleday. All rights reserved Scripture quotations marked NIV are taken from the Holy Bible, New International Version®. Copyright © 1973, 1978, 1984 by International Bible Society. Used by permission of Zondervan Bible Publishers. All rights reserved. Scripture quotations marked PHILLIPS are taken from The New Testament in Modern English, Revised Edition. Copyright © J. B. Phillips 1958, 1960, 1972. Used by permission of Macmillan Publishing Co., Inc. Scripture quotations marked RSV are taken from the Revised Standard Version. Copyright © 1946, 1952 by Division of Christian Education of the National Council of the Churches of Christ in the United States of America. Scripture quotations marked TLB are taken from The Living Bible. Copyright © 1971 by Tyndale House Publishers, Wheaton, Illinois 60187. All rights reserved. Scripture quotations marked WEY are taken from the Weymouth Bible. Scripture quotations marked ESV are from The English Standard Version. © 2001 by Crossway Bibles, a division of Good News Publishers. Scripture quotations marked NRSV are from the New Revised Standard Version of the Bible. © 1989 by the Division of Christian Education of the National Council of the Churches of Christ in the U.S.A. All rights reserved. Scripture quotations marked AMP are from The Amplified Bible: Old Testament. Copyright © 1962, 1964, 1965, 1987 by the Zondervan Corporation (used by permission); and The Amplified New Testament. Copyright © 1958 by the Lockman Foundation (used by permission). New American Standard Bible® © 1960, 1962, 1963, 1968, 1971, 1973, 1975, 1977, 1995 by The Lockman Foundation. New Testament and Revised Psalms copyright 1991, 1986, 1970 Confraternity of Christian Doctrine, Washington, D.C., and are used by the permission of the copyright owner. All rights reserved. The Good News Bible: The Bible in Today's English Version (TEV) © 1976 by the American Bible Society. Used by permission. Any italics in the Scripture quotations reflect the author's own emphasis.

ISBN 978-1-4041-9006-1

Printed in China
12 13 14 15 16 WAI 10 9 8

CONTENTS

Loved with a Steadfast Love

The steadfast love of the LORD never ceases, his mercies never come to an end; they are new every morning; great is thy faithfulness.

LOVED WITH A STEADFAST LOVE

Jeremiah was depressed, as gloomy as a giraffe with a neck ache. Jerusalem was under siege, his nation under duress. His world collapsed like a sand castle in a typhoon. He faulted God for his horrible emotional distress. He also blamed God for his physical ailments. "He [God] has made my flesh and my skin waste away, and broken my bones" (Lamentations 3:4 RSV).

His body ached. His heart was sick. His faith was puny. . . . He realized how fast he was sinking, so he shifted his gaze. "But this I call to mind, and therefore I have hope: The steadfast love of the LORD never ceases, his mercies never come to an end; they are new every morning; great is thy faithfulness. 'The LORD is my portion,' says my soul, 'therefore I will hope in him'" (vv. 21–24 RSV).

"But this I call to mind . . . " Depressed, Jeremiah altered his thoughts, shifted his attention. He turned his eyes away from his stormy world and looked into the wonder of God. He quickly recited a quintet of promises. (I can envision him tapping these out on the five fingers of his hand.)

1. The steadfast love of the Lord never ceases.
2. His mercies never come to an end.
3. They are new every morning.
4. Great is thy faithfulness.
5. The Lord is my portion.

The storm didn't cease, but his discouragement did.

—*FEARLESS*

Thank you, precious Savior, that your love is steadfast. Thank you that your mercies are new every morning. Thank you for your great faithfulness, not only to me but to all your people from the first day of creation. When I am tempted to become depressed and distressed, may I choose to gaze on you. May I remember that you are my portion. May I hope in your unceasing love, amen.

He is the living God, and steadfast forever; His kingdom is the one which shall not be destroyed, and His dominion shall endure to the end.

DANIEL 6:26

Trust me in your times of trouble, and I will rescue you,
and you will give me glory.

PSALM 50:15 NLT

PROBLEMS HAVE A PURPOSE

God will use whatever he wants to display his glory. Heavens and stars. History and nations. People and problems. My dying dad in West Texas.

The last three years of his life were scarred by ALS. The disease took him from a healthy mechanic to a bed-bound paralytic. He lost his voice and his muscles, but he never lost his faith. Visitors noticed. Not so much in what he said but more in what he didn't say. Never outwardly angry or bitter, Jack Lucado suffered stately.

His faith led one man to seek a like faith. After the funeral this man sought me out and told me. Because of my dad's example, he became a Jesus follower.

Did God orchestrate my father's illness for that very reason? Knowing the value he places on one soul, I wouldn't be surprised. And imagining the splendor of heaven, I know my father's not complaining.

A season of suffering is a small assignment when compared to the reward.

Rather than begrudge your problem, explore it. Ponder it. And most of all, use it. Use it to the glory of God. . . .

Your pain has a purpose. Your problems, struggles, heartaches, and hassles cooperate toward one end—the glory of God.

–It's Not About Me

Heavenly Father, when problems and pain come my way, help me to remember that nothing comes into my life without your approval. Rather than complain and cry about the challenges I face, help me consider them as opportunities to bring glory to you. Give me the strength and patience to bear my burdens in a way that will honor you. I will lift my eyes off the trials and keep them fixed firmly on you, amen.

Many are the afflictions of the righteous,
but the Lord delivers him out of them all.

Psalm 34:19

There is a wonderful joy ahead, even though you have to endure many trials for a little while. These trials will show that your faith is genuine. It is being tested as fire tests and purifies gold—though faith is far more precious than mere gold. So when your faith remains strong through many trials, it will bring you much praise and glory and honor on the day when Jesus Christ is revealed to the whole world.

1 Peter 1:6–7 nlt

*"Whoever compels you to go one mile, go with him two.
Give to him who asks you, and from him
who wants to borrow from you do not turn away."*

MATTHEW 5:41–42

THE SOCIETY OF THE SECOND MILE

Jesus created what we might deem the Society of the Second Mile. He presented a new option. Serve the ones who hate you; forgive the ones who hurt you. Take the lowest place, not the highest; seek to serve, not to be served. Retaliate, not in kind, but in kindness.

Roman soldiers could legally coerce Jewish citizens into carrying their load for one mile.[1] With nothing more than a command, they could requisition a farmer out of his field or a merchant out of his shop.

In such a case, Jesus said, "Give more than requested." Go two. At the end of one mile, keep going. Surprise the sandals off the soldier by saying, "I haven't done enough for you. I'm going a second mile." Do more than demanded. And do so with joy and grace!

The Society of the Second Mile still exists. . . . We have a second-mile servant in our church. By profession he is an architect. By passion, a servant. He arrives an hour or so prior to each worship service and makes his rounds through the men's restrooms. He wipes the sinks, cleans the mirrors, checks the toilets, and picks up paper off the floor. No one asked him to do the work; very few people are aware he does the work. He tells no one and requests nothing in return. He belongs to the Society of the Second Mile.

—EVERY DAY DESERVES A CHANCE

Lord Jesus, I want to live each day in a way that will please you. I know you are calling me to have a servant attitude: to take the lowest place and to seek to serve. When I am faced with a choice, may I choose to go the second mile no matter how difficult. And may I do so with joy and grace and a glad heart. Teach me to live a God-centered life that will bring honor to your name, amen.

Therefore, since we are receiving a kingdom which cannot be
shaken, let us have grace, by which we may serve God
acceptably with reverence and godly fear.

HEBREWS 12:28

He who heeds the word wisely will find good, and
whoever trusts in the LORD, happy is he.

PROVERBS 16:20

Forgetting those things which are behind and reaching
forward to those things which are ahead, I press toward the goal
for the prize of the upward call of God in Christ Jesus.
PHILIPPIANS 3:13–14

STAY IN THE RACE

In 1952, Florence Chadwick attempted to swim the chilly ocean waters between Catalina Island and the California shore. She swam through foggy weather and choppy seas for fifteen hours. Her muscles began to cramp, and her resolve weakened. She begged to be taken out of the water, but her mother, riding in a boat alongside, urged her not to give up. She kept trying but grew exhausted and stopped swimming. Aides lifted her out of the water and into the boat. They paddled a few more minutes, the mist broke, and she discovered that the shore was less than a half mile away. "All I could see was the fog," she explained at a news conference. "I think if I could have seen the shore, I would have made it."[2]

Take a long look at the shore that awaits you. Don't be fooled by the fog of the slump. The finish may be only strokes away. God may be, at this moment, lifting his hand to signal Gabriel to grab the trumpet. Angels may be assembling, saints gathering, demons trembling. Stay at it! Stay in the water. Stay in the race. Stay in the fight.

Give grace, one more time. Be generous, one more time. Teach one more class, encourage one more soul, swim one more stroke.

—*Facing Your Giants*

Father, you created us and you know everything there is to know about us. You know how discouraged we get at times and how we want to give up the struggles we face. Sometimes it seems as if we have more struggles than strength. We are tempted to quit. When that happens, Lord, remind us to endure for one more day, to be patient one more time, to serve without reward for one more season, amen.

Be strong and of good courage; do not be afraid, nor be dismayed, for the LORD your God is with you wherever you go.

JOSHUA 1:9

I have made, and I will bear; even I will carry, and will deliver you.

ISAIAH 46:4

He is a shield to those who put their trust in Him.

PROVERBS 30:5

The plans of the Lord stand firm forever.

Psalm 33:11 niv

Loved by an Unchanging God

God will always be the same.

No one else will. Lovers call you today and scorn you tomorrow. Companies follow pay raises with pink slips. Friends applaud you when you drive a classic and dismiss you when you drive a dud. Not God. God is "always the same" (Psalm 102:27 NLT).With him "there is no variation or shadow due to change" (James 1:17 ESV).

Catch God in a bad mood? Won't happen. Fear exhausting his grace? A sardine will swallow the Atlantic first. Think he's given up on you? Wrong. Did he not make a promise to you? "God is not a human being, and he will not lie. He is not a human, and he does not change his mind. What he says he will do, he does. What he promises, he makes come true" (Numbers 23:19 NCV). He's never sullen or sour, sulking or stressed. His strength, truth, ways, and love never change. He is "the same yesterday and today and forever" (Hebrews 13:8 ESV). And because he is, the Lord "will be the stability of your times" (Isaiah 33:6). . . .

God's plans will never change, because he makes his

plans in complete knowledge. Forget hopeful forecasting. He declares "the end from the beginning" (Isaiah 46:10 NASB). Nothing takes him by surprise. "The plans of the LORD stand firm forever" (Psalm 33:11 NIV).

The cross will not lose its power. The blood of Christ will not fade in strength. . . . "The LORD Almighty has spoken—who can change his plans? When his hand moves, who can stop him?" (Isaiah 14:27 NLT). God never changes.

–IT'S NOT ABOUT ME

Father God, it is such a comfort to know that you never change. Your grace and your love are inexhaustible. You are the same yesterday, today, and forever. You know the beginning of life to the end. Your power never grows weak, and your truth always stands firm. Your plans will never alter. You remain the same forever. We can count on your unfailing mercy. We praise your everlasting name, amen.

For I am the LORD, I do not change;
Therefore you are not consumed. . . .

MALACHI 3:6

Trust in the LORD forever, for in YAH,
the LORD, is everlasting strength.

ISAIAH 26:4

The LORD is my light and my salvation; whom shall I fear?
The LORD is the strength of my life; of whom shall I be afraid?

LIFE WITHOUT DOUBT AND DREAD

Fear, it seems, has taken a hundred-year lease on the building next door and set up shop. Oversized and rude, fear is unwilling to share the heart with happiness. Happiness complies and leaves. Do you ever see the two together? Can one be happy and afraid at the same time? Clear thinking and afraid? Confident and afraid? Merciful and afraid? No. Fear is the big bully in the high school hallway: brash, loud, and unproductive. . . . Fear herds us into a prison and slams the doors.

Wouldn't it be great to walk out?

Imagine your life wholly untouched by angst. What if faith, not fear, was your default reaction to threats? If you could hover a fear magnet over your heart and extract every last shaving of dread, insecurity, and doubt, what would remain? Envision a day, just one day, absent the dread of failure, rejection, and calamity. Can you imagine a life with no fear? This is the possibility behind Jesus' question.

"Why are you afraid?" he asks (Matthew 8:26 NCV).

—*FEARLESS*

I know, loving Father, that you do not want us to live in the dark dungeon of doubt and dread. You want us to live in the light of your loving faithfulness. Help us to remember your never-failing power and kindness. Teach us to release all doubt and dread from our minds. Let us live encouraged and free from all insecurity in the knowledge that you hold our lives together, amen.

Those who know Your name will put their trust in You;
for You, LORD, have not forsaken those who seek You.

PSALM 9:10

Do not fear, for I am with you; do not be dismayed,
for I am your God. I will strengthen you and help
you; I will uphold you in my righteous right hand.

ISAIAH 41:10 NIV

Devote yourselves to prayer with an alert mind and a thankful heart.
COLOSSIANS 4:2 NLT

A LIFE IMMERSED IN PRAYER

Most of us struggle with prayer. We forget to pray, and when we remember, we hurry through prayers with hollow words. Our minds drift; our thoughts scatter like a covey of quail. Why is this? Prayer requires minimal effort. No location is prescribed. No particular clothing is required. No title or office is stipulated. Yet you'd think we were wrestling a greased pig.

Speaking of pigs, Satan seeks to interrupt our prayers. Our battle with prayer is not entirely our fault. The devil knows the stories; he witnessed the angel in Peter's cell and the revival in Jerusalem. He knows what happens when we pray. "Our weapons have power from God that can destroy the enemy's strong places" (2 Corinthians 10:4 NCV).

Satan is not troubled when Max writes books or prepares sermons, but his knobby knees tremble when Max prays. Satan does not stutter or stumble when you walk through church doors or attend committee meetings. Demons aren't flustered when you read this book. But the walls of hell shake when one person with an honest heart and faithful confession says, "Oh, God, how great thou art."

Satan keeps you and me from prayer. He tries to position himself between us and God. But he scampers like a spooked dog when we move forward. So let's do.

"Humble yourselves before God. Resist the devil, and he will flee from you. Draw close to God, and God will draw close to you" (James 4:7–8 NLT).

Jesus immersed his words and work in prayer. Powerful things happen when we do the same.

–Outlive Your Life

Gracious Lord, you have opened for us the throne room of heaven. We can come into your very presence with our petitions and praise. As you immersed your life in prayer, so may we make prayer a priority each day. May we never forget what a privilege it is to speak freely and openly to you any time and any place. You are always listening, amen.

The eyes of the Lord are on the righteous,
and His ears are open to their prayers.

1 Peter 3:12

I say to you, whatever things you ask when you pray,
believe that you receive them, and you will have them.

Mark 11:24

"Don't be afraid; just believe."
MARK 5:36 NIV

LOVED BY A GOD YOU CAN TRUST

The presence of fear does not mean you have no faith. Fear visits everyone. Even Christ was afraid (Mark 14:33). But make your fear a visitor and not a resident. Hasn't fear taken enough? Enough smiles? Chuckles? Restful nights, exuberant days? Meet your fears with faith.

Do what my father urged my brother and me to do. Summertime for the Lucado family always involved a trip from West Texas to the Rocky Mountains. (Think Purgatory to Paradise.) My dad loved to fish for trout on the edge of the white-water rivers. Yet he knew that the currents were dangerous and his sons could be careless. Upon arrival we'd scout out the safe places to cross the river. He'd walk us down the bank until we found a line of stable rocks. He was even known to add one or two to compensate for our short strides.

As we watched, he'd test the stones, knowing if they held him, they'd hold us. Once on the other side, he'd signal for us to follow.

"Don't be afraid," he could have said. "Trust me."

We children never needed coaxing. But we adults often do. Does a river of fear run between you and Jesus? Cross over to him.

Believe he can. Believe he cares.

–Every Day Deserves a Chance

Dear God, you have promised to walk life's path before us and show us the way. You don't leave us to find our way alone. Even when the path looks uncertain and frightening, help us focus on you and your promise. Your presence strengthens us. You are a God we can depend on. You are our strong defender, amen.

The Lord is my strength and my shield;
my heart trusted in Him, and I am helped.

Psalm 28:7

Blessed is the man who trusts in the Lord, and whose
hope is the Lord. For he shall be like a tree planted by the waters,
which spreads out its roots by the river.

Jeremiah 17:7–8

You [O God] are the same, and Your years will have no end.

PSALM 102:27

LOVED BY AN ETERNAL GOD

Life . . . is a cache of moments: measurable and count-able increments, like change in a pocket or buttons in a can. Your pocket may be full of decades, my pocket may be down to a few years, but everyone has a certain num-ber of moments.

Everyone, that is, except God. As we list the mind-stretching claims of Christ, let's include this one near the top. "Before Abraham was born, I am" (John 8:58 NASB).

Scripture broadcasts this attribute in surround sound. God is "from everlasting" (Psalm 93:2) and the "everlasting King" (Jeremiah 10:10). . . . You'll more quickly measure the salt of the ocean than measure the existence of God because "the number of His years is unsearchable" (Job 36:26 NASB).

Trace the tree back to a seed. Trace the dress back to a factory. Trace the baby back to a mommy. Trace God back to . . . to . . . to . . .

No one. Not even God made God. "From eternity I am He" (Isaiah 43:13 NASB).

He is eternal. He does not live sequential moments, laid out on a time line, one following the other. His world is one moment, or better stated, momentless. He doesn't view history as a progression of centuries but as a single photo. He captures your life, your entire life, in one glance. He sees your birth and burial in one frame. He knows your beginning and your end because he has neither.

–It's Not About Me

Dear God, you are our eternal Father. You have always been and will always be. When unexpected events occur, may we remember that nothing surprises you. You know the beginning of all things to the end. And our lives are in your care, amen.

Now to the King eternal, immortal, invisible, to God who alone is wise, be honor and glory forever and ever. Amen.

1 Timothy 1:17

For the Lord is good; His mercy is everlasting, and His truth endures to all generations.

Psalm 100:5

To everything there is a season, a time for every purpose under heaven.

FACING THE FUTURE WITH GOD

What person passes through life surprise free? If you don't want change, go to a soda machine; that's the only place you won't find any. Remember the summary of Solomon? "To everything there is a season, a time for every purpose under heaven" (Ecclesiastes 3:1) . . .

God dispenses life the way he manages his cosmos: through seasons. When it comes to the earth, we understand God's management strategy. Nature needs winter to rest and spring to awaken. We don't dash into underground shelters at the sight of spring's tree buds. Autumn colors don't prompt warning sirens. Earthly seasons don't upset us. But unexpected personal ones certainly do. . . .

Are you on the eve of change? Do you find yourself looking into a new chapter? Is the foliage of your world showing signs of a new season? Heaven's message for you is clear: when everything else changes, God's presence never does. You journey in the company of the Holy Spirit, who "will teach you everything and will remind you of everything I myself have told you" (John 14:26 NLT).

So make friends with whatever's next.

Embrace it. Accept it. Don't resist it. Change is not only a part of life; change is a necessary part of God's strategy. To use us to change the world, he alters our assignments. Gideon: from farmer to general; Mary: from peasant girl to the mother of Christ; Paul: from local rabbi to world evangelist. God transitioned Joseph from a baby brother to an Egyptian prince. He changed David from a shepherd to a king. Peter wanted to fish the Sea of Galilee. God called him to lead the first church. God makes reassignments.

But he wants you to know: you'll never face the future without his help.

—FEARLESS

Father God, you know how frightening the future can be, with unexpected twists and turns in the road of life. Help us remember that you ordain the days of our lives. You assign each stage of the journey, but you walk the path with us, amen.

The steps of a good man are ordered by the LORD, and He delights in his way. Though he fall, he shall not be utterly cast down; for the LORD upholds him with His hand.

PSALM 37:23–24

We use God's mighty weapons, not mere worldly weapons,
to knock down the Devil's strongholds.

2 CORINTHIANS 10:4 NLT

HELP FOR PREVAILING PROBLEMS

Does one prevailing problem leech your life?

Some are prone to cheat. Others, quick to doubt. Maybe you worry. Yes, everyone worries some, but you own the national distributorship of anxiety. Perhaps you are judgmental. Sure, everybody can be critical, but you pass more judgments than a federal judge.

What is that one weakness, bad habit, rotten attitude? Where does Satan have a stronghold within you? Ahh, there is the fitting word—*stronghold*: a fortress, citadel, thick walls, tall gates. It's as if the devil staked a claim on one weakness and constructed a rampart around it.

Strongholds: old, difficult, discouraging challenges.

That's what David faced when he looked at Jerusalem. . . .

Nevertheless.

"Nevertheless, David took the stronghold" (2 Samuel 5:9 ESV).

Granted, the city was old. The walls were difficult. The voices were discouraging . . . *Nevertheless*, David took the stronghold.

Wouldn't you love for God to write a *nevertheless* in your biography? Born to alcoholics, *nevertheless* she led a sober life. Never went to college, *nevertheless* he mastered a trade. Didn't read the Bible until retirement age, *nevertheless* he came to a deep and abiding faith.

We all need a *nevertheless*. And God has plenty to go around. Strongholds mean nothing to him. Remember Paul's words? "We use God's mighty weapons, not mere worldly weapons, to knock down the Devil's strongholds" (2 Corinthians 10:4 NLT).

You and I fight with toothpicks; God comes with battering rams and cannons. What he did for David, he can do for us.

—*FACING YOUR GIANTS*

Blessed Father, as you helped David conquer a stronghold, so you can help us conquer the strongholds in our lives. You have promised freedom and victory. Father, will you break these strongholds with your mighty power? You steady us with your love, amen.

Call upon Me in the day of trouble;
I will deliver you, and you shall glorify Me.

PSALM 50:15

I will make all My goodness pass before you, and
I will proclaim the name of the LORD before you.

EXODUS 33:19

A GLIMPSE OF GOD'S GLORY

God places his servant in the cleft of a rock, telling Moses: "You cannot see My face; for no man shall see Me, and live. . . . I . . . will cover you with My hand while I pass by. Then I will take away My hand, and you shall see My back; but My face shall not be seen" (Exodus 33:20, 22–23).

And so Moses, cowering beneath the umbrella of God's palm, waits, surely with face bowed, eyes covered, and pulse racing, until God gives the signal. When the hand lifts, Moses' eyes do the same and catch a distant, disappearing glance of the back parts of God. The heart and center of the Maker is too much for Moses to bear. A fading glimpse will have to do. I'm seeing the long gray hair of Moses wind-whipped forward and his leathery hand grabbing a rock in the wall lest he fall. And as the gust settles and his locks rest again on his shoulders, we see the impact. His face. Gleaming. Bright as if backlit by a thousand torches. Unknown to Moses, but undeniable to the Hebrews, is his shimmering face. When he descended the mountain, "the sons of Israel could not look intently at the face of Moses because of the glory of his face" (2 Corinthians 3:7 NASB).

Witnesses saw not anger in his jaw, or worry in his eyes, or a scowl on his lips; they saw God's glory in his face.

Did he have reason for anger? Cause for worry? Of course. Challenges await him. A desert and forty years of great challenges. But now, having seen God's face, he can face them. . . .

You and I need what Moses needed—a glimpse of God's glory.

–*It's Not About Me*

Heavenly Father, you are glorious and mighty in all you do. Sunsets preview your glory. Newborn babies prove your tenderness. The kindness of the Savior demonstrates your power. Thank you, Lord, for these glimpses of your glory, amen.

Now to Him who is able to do exceedingly
abundantly above all that we ask or think, according
to the power that works in us, to Him be glory.

Ephesians 3:20–21

We have access by faith into this grace in which we stand,
and rejoice in hope of the glory of God.

Romans 5:2

God will wipe away every tear . . . there shall be no more death,
nor sorrow, nor crying . . . for the former things have passed away.

REVELATION 21:4

ASSIGNMENTS IN HEAVEN

You won't be bored in heaven because you won't be the same you in heaven. Boredom emerges from soils that heaven disallows. The soil of weariness: our eyes tire. Mental limitations: information overload dulls us. Self-centeredness: we grow disinterested when the spotlight shifts to others. Tedium: meaningless activity siphons vigor.

But Satan will take these weedy soils to hell with him, leaving you with a keen mind, endless focus, and God-honoring assignments.

Yes, you will have assignments in heaven. God gave Adam and Eve garden responsibilities. "Let them have dominion" (Genesis 1:26). He mantled the couple with leadership "over the fish of the sea, over the birds of the air, and over the cattle, over all the earth and over every creeping thing that creeps on the earth" (v. 26). Adam was placed in the garden "to tend and keep it" (2:15).

Adam and his descendants will do it again. "[God's] servants shall serve Him" (Revelation 22:3). What is service if not responsible activity? Those who are faithful over a few things will rule over many (Matthew 25:21 NIV).

You might oversee the orbit of a distant planetary system . . . design a mural in the new city . . . monitor the expansion of a new species of plants or animals. "Of the increase of His government and peace there will be no end" (Isaiah 9:7). God's new world will be marked by increase. Increased planets? Colors? Music? Seems likely. What does a creator do but create?

What do his happy children do but serve him?

—*3:16: THE NUMBERS OF HOPE*

Lord, you have promised that those who believe in you will live with you forever in heaven. Thank you for the promise of heaven. We will serve you there with great joy and gladness, amen.

The Lord will deliver me from every evil work
and preserve me for His heavenly kingdom.

2 TIMOTHY 4:18

*"I have suffered the loss of all things, and count
them as rubbish, that I may gain Christ."*

PHILIPPIANS 3:8

LOVED BY A FAITHFUL GOD

Peer through the small window in the wall of the Roman jail. See the man in chains? The aging fellow with the stooped shoulders and hawkish nose? That's Paul, the imprisoned apostle. His chains never come off. The guards never leave. And he's probably wondering if he'll ever get out. . . .

By the time we find Paul in his cell, he has been beaten, lied about, storm tossed, rejected, and neglected.

Ah, but at least he has the church. At least he can take comfort in the thought of the unified Roman congregation he helped strengthen, right? Hardly. The Roman church is in trouble. . . . Power-hungry preachers occupy the parsonage. You expect such antics out of nonbelievers, but Christians preaching for personal gain? Paul is facing Prozac-level problems. . . .

And who knows what Emperor Nero will do? He feeds disciples to the lions for lunch. Does Paul have any guarantee the same won't happen to him? . . . Paul is not naive. He knows that the only thing between him and death is a nod from moody Nero. Paul has every reason to be stressed out. . . .

But he isn't. Rather than count the bricks of his prison, he plants a garden within it. He itemizes not the mistreatments of people, but the faithfulness of God.

"I want you to know, brethren that what has happened to me has really served to advance the gospel" (Philippians 1:12 RSV). He may appear to be bumped off track, but he is actually right on target. Why? One reason. Christ is preached. The mission is being accomplished.

—EVERY DAY DESERVES A CHANCE

Father, earthly stress and struggles remind us of your faithfulness. Help us, Lord, to serve you without grumbling. May we, like the apostle Paul, choose to plant a garden in the bricks of our "prison." Help plant our thoughts firmly on your faithfulness. All hope comes from you, amen.

Let your heart therefore be loyal to the LORD our God, to walk in His statutes and keep His commandments, as at this day.

1 KINGS 8:61

"But seek first the kingdom of God and His righteousness, and all these things shall be added to you."

MATTHEW 6:33

He is in charge of it all, has the final word on everything.
At the center of all this, Christ rules the church.
EPHESIANS 1:22 MSG

THE CENTER OF THE UNIVERSE

Tapping the collective shoulder of humanity, God points to the Son—his Son—and says, "Behold the center of it all."

> God raised him [Christ] from death and set him on a throne in deep heaven, in charge of running the universe, everything from galaxies to governments, no name and no power exempt from his rule. And not just for the time being, but forever. He is in charge of it all, has the final word on everything. At the center of all this, Christ rules the church. (Ephesians 1:20–22 MSG)

When God looks at the center of the universe, he doesn't look at you. When heaven's stagehands direct the spotlight toward the star of the show, I need no sunglasses. No light falls on me.

Lesser orbs, that's us. Appreciated. Valued. Loved dearly. But central? Essential? Pivotal? Nope. Sorry. . . . The world does not revolve around us. Our comfort is not God's priority. If it is, something's gone awry. If we are the marquee event, how do we explain flat-earth challenges like death, disease, slumping economies, or rumbling earthquakes? If God exists to please us, then shouldn't we always be pleased?

Could a Copernican shift be in order? Perhaps our place is not at the center of the universe. God does not exist to make a big deal out of us. We exist to make a big deal out of him. It's not about you. It's not about me. It's all about him.

–It's Not About Me

Heavenly Father, we praise you, King of heaven. You are great above all. You are gracious and we are grateful. We love you, adore you. We worship you and thank you for the gift of your Son, amen.

Ascribe to the LORD the glory due his name;
worship the LORD in the splendor of his holiness.

PSALM 29:2 NIV

O LORD, how manifold are Your works! In wisdom You
have made them all. The earth is full of Your possessions.

PSALM 104:24

We are God's masterpiece. He has created us anew in Christ Jesus,
so that we can do the good things he planned for us long ago.

CREATED TO DO GREAT WORKS

By the time you knew what to call it, you were neck deep in it. It's called life. And this one is yours.

Complete with summers and songs and gray skies and tears, you have a life. Didn't request one, but you have one. A first day. A final day. And a few thousand in between. You've been given an honest-to-goodness human life.

You've been given your life. No one else has your version. You'll never bump into yourself on the sidewalk. You'll never meet anyone who has your exact blend of lineage, loves, and longings. Your life will never be lived by anyone else. You're not a jacket in an attic that can be recycled after you are gone.

Life is racing by, and if we aren't careful, you and I will look up, and our shot at it will have passed us by. Some people don't bother with such thoughts. They grind through their days without lifting their eyes to look. They live and die and never ask why.

But you aren't numbered among them. It's not enough for you to do well. You want to do good. You want your life to matter. You want to live in such a way that the world will be glad you did. . . .

We are given a choice . . . an opportunity to make a big difference during a difficult time. What if we did? What if we rocked the world with hope? Infiltrated all corners with God's love and life?

We are created by a great God to do great works.

–OUTLIVE YOUR LIFE

Heavenly Father, thank you for giving us life and for creating us to be unique among all the people of the world. May the moments and days of our lives bring honor to you, the Giver of life. Teach us your perfect path, and guide us to do your will. Open our eyes and hearts to infiltrate our corner of the world with your love and life, amen.

God is able to make all grace abound toward you,
that you, always having all sufficiency in all things,
may have an abundance for every good work.

2 CORINTHIANS 9:8

He has delivered us from such a deadly peril, and he will
deliver us. On him we have set our hope that he will
continue to deliver us, as you help us by your prayers.

2 CORINTHIANS 1:10–11 NIV

GOD'S FINEST WORK

Peter and his fellow storm riders knew they were in trouble. "But the boat was now in the middle of the sea, tossed by the waves, for the wind was contrary" (Matthew 14:24).

What should have been a sixty-minute cruise became a nightlong battle. The boat lurched and lunged like a kite in a March wind. Sunlight was a distant memory. Rain fell from the night sky in buckets. Lightning sliced the blackness with a silver sword. Winds whipped the sails, leaving the disciples "in the middle of the sea, tossed by the waves." Apt description, perhaps, for your stage in life? Perhaps all we need to do is substitute a couple of nouns . . .

In the middle of a divorce, tossed about by guilt.

In the middle of debt, tossed about by creditors.

In the middle of a recession, tossed about by stimulus packages and bailouts.

The disciples fought the storm for nine cold, skin-drenching hours. And about 4:00 a.m., the unspeakable happened. They spotted someone coming on the water.

"'A ghost!' they said, crying out in terror" (Matthew 14:26 MSG).

They didn't expect Jesus to come to them this way.

Neither do we. We expect him to come in the form of peaceful hymns or Easter Sundays or quiet retreats. We expect to find Jesus in morning devotionals, church suppers, and meditation. We never expect to see him in a bear market, pink slip, lawsuit, foreclosure, or war. We never expect to see him in a storm. But it is in storms that he does his finest work, for it is in storms that he has our keenest attention.

—FEARLESS

Lord, we cannot control the storms of life, but we can control where we look in the storm. We choose to look to you. We choose to see you in the middle of our heartbreaks and health crises. When we are tossed about by the trials and temptations of life, remind us not to be overwhelmed by fear and doubt, but to look for your calming presence, amen.

He got up and rebuked the wind and the raging waters; the storm subsided, and all was calm. "Where is your faith?" he asked his disciples. In fear and amazement they asked one another, "who is this? He commands even the winds and the water, and they obey him."

LUKE 8:24–25 NIV

*"God will help you deal with whatever
hard things come up when the time comes."*
Matthew 6:34 msg

Worry Dishonors God

You look at tomorrow's demands, next week's bills, next month's silent calendar. Your future looks as barren as the Sinai Desert. "How can I face my future?" . . .

God knows what you need and where you'll be. . . . Trust him. "Give your entire attention to what God is doing right now, and don't get worked up about what may or may not happen tomorrow. God will help you deal with whatever hard things come up when the time comes" (Matthew 6:34 msg).

The Greek word for *worry*, *merimnao*, stems from the verb *merizo* (divide) and *nous* (mind). Worry cleavers the mind, splitting thoughts between today and tomorrow. Today stands no chance against it. Fretting over tomorrow's problems today siphons the strength you need for now, leaving you anemic and weak.

Worry gives small problems big shadows. Montaigne said, "My life has been full of terrible misfortunes, most of which never happened."[3] Corrie ten Boom commented, "Worry does not empty tomorrow of its sorrows;

it empties today of its strength."[4] Worry scuttles our lives, hurts us, and most sadly, dishonors God.

—*Every Day Deserves a Chance*

Father, when demands or disasters come our way, help us trust you. Help us trust you to guide us safely through the storms of life. Help us turn to you for guidance when we feel lost and confused. Most of all, help us remember your loving faithfulness that has never failed, amen.

In all these things we are more than conquerors
through Him who loved us.

Romans 8:37

A man's heart plans his way, but the Lord directs his steps.

Proverbs 16:9

For You are my lamp, O Lord;
the Lord shall enlighten my darkness.

2 Samuel 22:29

Men shall speak of the might of Your awesome acts,
and I will declare Your greatness.

GOD'S PROMISES ARE UNENDING

Know this: God, your God, is God indeed, a God you can depend upon. He keeps his covenant of loyal love with those who love him and observe his commandments for a thousand generations" (Deuteronomy 7:9 MSG).

God makes and never breaks his promises. The Hebrew word for *covenant, beriyth,* means "a solemn agreement with binding force."[5] His irrevocable covenant runs like a scarlet thread through the tapestry of Scripture. Remember his promise to Noah?

> "I establish my covenant with you: Never again will all life be cut off by the waters of a flood; never again will there be a flood to destroy the earth."
>
> And God said, "This is the sign of the covenant I am making between me and you and every living creature with you, a covenant for all generations to come: I have set my rainbow in the clouds, and it will be the sign of the covenant between me and the earth." (Genesis 9:11–13 NIV)

Every rainbow reminds us of God's covenant. Curiously, astronauts who've seen rainbows from outer space tell us they form a complete circle.[6] God's promises are equally unbroken and unending.

–*Facing Your Giants*

Heavenly Father, your word tells us that not one of your promises has ever failed. You are a covenant God who is steadfast and true. We can count on every word you have spoken. We can rely on you to answer our prayers as you have promised. We can stand firm on the truths of your word, amen.

Therefore know that the LORD your God, He is God, the faithful God
who keeps covenant and mercy for a thousand generations
with those who love Him and keep His commandments.

DEUTERONOMY 7:9

Blessed be the LORD, who has given . . . according to all that He
promised. There has not failed one word of all His good promise.

1 KINGS 8:56

"For God so loved the world that he gave his one and only Son,
that whoever believes in him shall not perish but have eternal life."
JOHN 3:16 NIV

GOD'S GRACIOUS LOVE

The heart of the human problem is the heart of the human. And God's treatment is prescribed in John 3:16.

He loves. He gave.

We believe. We live.

The words are to Scripture what the Mississippi River is to America—an entryway into the heartland. Believe or dismiss them, embrace or reject them, any serious consideration of Christ must include them. Would a British historian dismiss the Magna Carta? Egyptologists overlook the Rosetta stone? Could you ponder the words of Christ and never immerse yourself into John 3:16?

The verse is an alphabet of grace, a table of contents to the Christian hope, each word a safe-deposit box of jewels. Read it again, slowly and aloud, and note the word that snatches your attention. . . .

"God so *loved* the world . . ." We'd expect an anger-fueled God. One who punishes the world, recycles the world, forsakes the world . . . but loves the world?

The *world*? This world? Heartbreakers, hope snatchers, and dream dousers prowl this orb. Dictators rage. Abusers inflict. Reverends think they deserve the title. But God loves. And he loves the world so much he gave his: Declarations? Rules? Dicta? Edicts?

No. The heart-stilling, mind-bending, deal-making-or-breaking claim of John 3:16 is this: *God gave his Son . . . his only Son*. No abstract ideas, but a flesh-wrapped divinity. Scripture equates Jesus with God. God, then, gave himself. Why? So that "*whoever* believes in him shall not perish."

—3:16: The Numbers of Hope

Father God, your love is truly beyond understanding. It reaches out to every person in every corner of the world. It is offered freely to all people. It is a gracious, merciful, and patient love. May we be willing to spread the good news of your love far and wide. Teach us to talk to everyone about your mighty works, amen.

But God, who is rich in mercy, because of His great love with which He loved us, even when we were dead in trespasses, made us alive together with Christ.

Ephesians 2:4–5

We love Him because He first loved us.

1 John 4:19

Always be joyful. Pray continually, and give thanks whatever happens. That is what God wants for you in Christ Jesus.

1 THESSALONIANS 5:16—18 NCV

GRATITUDE IS ALWAYS AN OPTION

If you look long enough and hard enough, you'll find something to bellyache about. So quit looking! Lift your eyes off the weeds. Major in the grace of God. And . . .

Measure the gifts of God. Collect your blessings. Catalog his kindnesses. Assemble your reasons for gratitude and recite them. "Always be joyful. Pray continually, and give thanks whatever happens. That is what God wants for you in Christ Jesus" (1 Thessalonians 5:16–18 NCV).

Look at the totality of those terms. *Always be joyful. Pray continually. Give thanks whatever happens.* Learn a lesson from Sidney Connell. When her brand-new bicycle was stolen, she called her dad with the bad news. He expected his daughter to be upset. But Sidney wasn't crying. She was honored. "Dad," she boasted, "out of all the bikes they could have taken, they took mine."

Gratitude is always an option. Matthew Henry made it his. When the famous scholar was accosted by thieves and robbed of his purse, he wrote this in his diary: "Let me be thankful first, because I was never robbed before;

second, because, although they took my purse, they did not take my life; third, although they took my all, it was not much; and, fourthly, because it was I who was robbed, not I who robbed."[7]

Make gratitude your default emotion, and you'll find yourself giving thanks for the problems of life.

—EVERY DAY DESERVES A CHANCE

Dear Lord, your generosity to us is amazing. Your blessings are countless. Your kindness is a breath of fresh air. We choose to be grateful and joyful no matter what today brings. We choose to make gratitude our default emotion. We give thanks to you for all things, amen.

Oh, give thanks to the LORD, for He is good!
For His mercy endures forever.

PSALM 136:1

You shall eat in plenty and be satisfied, and praise the name of
the LORD your God, who has dealt wondrously with you.

JOEL 2:26

"Do not worry about your life. . . . Do not seek what you should eat or what you should drink, nor have an anxious mind."

LUKE 12:22, 29

LOVED BY THE GREAT GIVER

Accumulation of wealth is a popular defense against fear. Since we fear losing our jobs, health care, or retirement benefits, we amass possessions, thinking the more we have, the safer we are. . . .

We engineer stock and investment levies, take cover behind the hedge of hedge funds. We trust annuities and pensions to the point that balance statements determine our mood levels. But then come the Katrina-level recessions and downturns, and the confusion begins all over again. . . .

If there were no God, stuff-trusting would be the only appropriate response to an uncertain future. But there is a God. And this God does not want his children to trust money. . . .

Scrooge didn't create the world; God did.

Psalm 104 celebrates this lavish creation with twenty-three verses of itemized blessings: the heavens and the earth, the waters and streams and trees and birds and goats and wine and oil and bread and people and lions. God is the source of "innumerable teeming things, living things both small and great. . . . These all wait for You, that You may give them their food in due season" (vv. 25, 27).

And he does. God is the great giver. The great provider. The fount of every blessing. Absolutely generous and utterly dependable. The resounding and recurring message of Scripture is clear: God owns it all. God shares it all. Trust him, not stuff!

—*FEARLESS*

Loving Father, we praise you for your generosity and your mighty power. The majesty of your creation is amazing. Your provision of our needs is humbling. How good you are to your children! May we never trust in earthly provisions rather than in you, the great provider. You guide your people wisely and well, amen.

The everlasting God, the LORD, the Creator of the ends of the earth, neither faints nor is weary. His understanding is unsearchable.

ISAIAH 40:28

Blessed be the LORD God of Israel, who has fulfilled with His hands what He spoke with His mouth.

2 CHRONICLES 6:4

The battle is the Lord's. . . .

1 SAMUEL 17:47

TAKE A SWING AT YOUR GIANT

David . . . runs toward the army to meet Goliath (1 Samuel 17:48). . . .

Goliath throws back his head in laughter, just enough to shift his helmet and expose a square inch of forehead flesh. David spots the target and seizes the moment. The sound of the swirling sling is the only sound in the valley. *Ssshhww. Ssshhww. Ssshhww.* The stone torpedoes through the air and into the skull; Goliath's eyes cross and legs buckle. He crumples to the ground and dies. David runs over and yanks Goliath's sword from its sheath, shish-kebabs the Philistine, and cuts off his head.

You might say that David knew how to get *a head* of his giant.

When was the last time you did the same? How long since you ran toward your challenge? We tend to retreat, duck behind a desk of work or crawl into a nightclub of distraction or a bed of forbidden love. For a moment, a day, or a year, we feel safe, insulated, anesthetized, but then the work runs out, the liquor wears off, or the lover leaves, and we hear Goliath again. Booming. Bombastic.

Try a different tack. Rush your giant with a God-saturated soul. *Giant of divorce, you aren't entering my home! Giant of depression? It may take a lifetime, but you won't conquer me. Giant of alcohol, bigotry, child abuse, insecurity . . . you're going down.* How long since you loaded your sling and took a swing at your giant?

—FACING YOUR GIANTS

Gracious God, there are days when we feel surrounded by giants. Insecurities and doubts and worries flood our minds. But your mighty power instills confidence to confront every giant in life. Saturate our souls with your word. Remind us to look at every obstacle through your power and your might. May we be victorious through your holy name, amen.

❧❦❧

In the day when I cried out, You answered me,
and made me bold with strength in my soul.

PSALM 138:3

God is my strength and power, and He makes my way perfect.

2 SAMUEL 22:33

Silver and gold I do not have, but what I do have I give you:
In the name of Jesus Christ of Nazareth, rise up and walk.

WORKS DONE IN GOD'S NAME

A gate called Beautiful. The man was anything but.

He couldn't walk but had to drag himself about on his knees. He passed his days among the contingent of real and pretend beggars who coveted the coins of the worshippers entering Solomon's court.

Peter and John were among them.

The needy man saw the apostles, lifted his voice, and begged for money. They had none to give, yet still they stopped. "Peter and John looked straight at him and said, 'Look at us!'" (Acts 3:4 NCV).

Then Peter said, "Silver and gold I do not have, but what I do have I give you: In the name of Jesus Christ of Nazareth, rise up and walk" (v. 6).

The thick, meaty hand of the fisherman reached for the frail, thin one of the beggar. Think Sistine Chapel and the high hand of God. One from above, the other from below. A holy helping hand. Peter lifted the man toward himself. The cripple swayed like a newborn calf finding its balance. It appeared as if the man would fall, but he didn't. He stood. And as he stood, he began to shout, and passersby began to stop. They stopped and watched the cripple skip.

An honest look led to a helping hand that led to a conversation about eternity. Works done in God's name long outlive our earthly lives.

Let's be the people who stop at the gate. Let's look at the hurting until we hurt with them. No hurrying past, turning away, or shifting of eyes. No pretending or glossing over. Let's look at the face until we see the person.

—Outlive Your Life

Lord, there are so many people whose needs can only be healed by your gracious love. When we see people in need, help us not to rush by but to stop and lend a helping hand. Open our eyes to see the hurting and soften our hearts to hurt with them. Let us learn from your example how to reach out in loving compassion to help those in need, amen.

Be kind to one another, tenderhearted, forgiving
one another, even as God in Christ forgave you.

Ephesians 4:32

Be of good comfort, be of one mind, live in peace;
and the God of love and peace will be with you.

2 Corinthians 13:11

Why are you cast down, O my soul? . . . Hope in God.
PSALM 42:11

FACE YOUR FEARS BY FACING GOD

"I look at this people—oh! what a stubborn, hard-headed people!" (Exodus 32:9 MSG). God spoke these words to Moses on Mount Sinai. The disloyalty of the calf-worshipping Hebrews stunned God. He had given them a mayor's-seat perch at his Exodus extravaganza. They saw water transform into blood, high noon change to a midnight sky, the Red Sea turn into a red carpet, and the Egyptian army become fish bait. God gave manna with the morning dew, quail with the evening sun. He earned their trust. . . .

And yet, when God called Moses to a summit meeting, the people panicked like henless chicks. "They rallied around Aaron and said, 'Do something. Make gods for us who will lead us. That Moses, the man who got us out of Egypt—who knows what's happened to him?'" (Exodus 32:1 MSG).

The scurvy of fear infected everyone in the camp. They crafted a metal cow and talked to it. . . .

Note: the presence of fear in the Hebrews didn't bother God; their response to it did. Nothing persuaded the people to trust him. Plagues didn't. Liberation from slavery didn't. God shed light on their path and dropped food in their laps, and still they didn't believe him. Nothing penetrated their hearts. . . .

More than three thousand years removed, we understand God's frustration. Turn to a statue for help? How stupid. Face your fears by facing a cow? Udderly foolish!

We opt for more sophisticated therapies: belly-stretching food binges or budget-busting shopping sprees. We bow before a whiskey bottle or lose ourselves in an eighty-hour workweek. Progress? Hardly. We still face fears without facing God.

—3:16: The Numbers of Hope

Loving Father, you know how weak and frail we are when faced with fears. We tend to turn to things and people for answers and solutions to life's problems rather than turn to you. Or we try to work out solutions in our own feeble strength, when you are eager to provide the solution for us. Forgive us when we disappoint you, Father. May we always turn first to you, amen.

You are my hope, O Lord GOD; You are my trust from my youth.

PSALM 71:5

Blessed is that man who makes the LORD his trust.

PSALM 40:4

"You will hear of wars and rumors of wars. See that you are not troubled; for all these things must come to pass, but the end is not yet."

MATTHEW 24:6

LOVED BY A TRUSTWORTHY GOD

Nature is a pregnant creation, third-trimester heavy. When a tornado rips through a city in Kansas or an earthquake flattens a region in Pakistan, this is more than barometric changes or shifts of ancient fault lines. The universe is passing through the final hours before delivery. Painful contractions are in the forecast.

As are conflicts: "wars and rumors of wars." One nation invading another. One superpower defying another. Borders will always need checkpoints. War correspondents will always have employment. The population of the world will never see peace this side of heaven.

Christians will suffer the most. "Then you will be handed over to be persecuted and put to death, and you will be hated by all nations because of me" (v. 9 NIV).

But remember: "All these [challenging times] are the beginning of birth pains" (v. 8 NIV), and birth pangs aren't all bad. (Easy for me to say.) Birth pains signal the onset of the final push. The obstetrician assures the mom-to-be, "It's going to hurt for a time, but it's going to get better." Jesus assures us of the same. Global conflicts indicate our date on the maternity calendar. We are in the final hours, just a few pushes from delivery, a few brief ticks of eternity's clock from the great crowning of creation. A whole new world is coming! . . .

All things, big and small, flow out of the purpose of God and serve his good will. When the world appears out of control, it isn't. When warmongers appear to be in charge, they aren't. When ecological catastrophes dominate the day, don't let them dominate you.

Let's trust our heavenly Father.

—*FEARLESS*

Glorious God, all things flow out of your purposes. You are in control even when catastrophes dominate the day. When global conflicts increase, may we remember that these are birth pangs preparing the way for a whole new wonderful world. May we lay aside all anxiety and fear and see these singular events as signs for rejoicing and anticipating your peaceful kingdom, amen.

Though a host encamp against me, my heart shall not fear;
though war arise against me, yet I will be confident.

PSALM 27:3 RSV

Be strong in the Lord and in the power of His might.

EPHESIANS 6:10

Call upon Me in the day of trouble;
I will deliver you, and you shall glorify Me.

ONE GOOD DAY AT A TIME

Rejoice *in* this day? God invites us to. As Paul rejoiced *in* prison; David wrote psalms *in* the wilderness; Jonah prayed *in* the fish belly; Paul and Silas sang *in* jail; Shadrach, Meshach, and Abednego remained resolute *in* the fiery furnace; John saw heaven *in* his exile; and Jesus prayed *in* his garden of pain . . . Could we rejoice smack-dab *in* the midst of this day?

Imagine the difference if we could.

Suppose neck deep in a terrible . . . day you resolve to give it a chance. You choose not to drink or work or worry it away but give it a fair shake. You trust more. Stress less. Amplify gratitude. Mute grumbling. And what do you know? Before long the day is done and surprisingly decent.

So decent, in fact, that you resolve to give the next day the same fighting chance. It arrives with its hang-ups and bang-ups, bird drops and shirt stains, but by and large, by golly, giving the day a chance works! You do the same the next day and the next. Days become a week. Weeks become months. Months become years of good days.

In such a fashion good lives are built. One good day at a time.

Wonderful Savior, each day is a gift from you. It is an opportunity to bring glory to you. We can do that by rejoicing in the circumstances that come our way today, and the next day, and the day after that. Give us strength to praise you and be joyful no matter how difficult the day. May our joy bring joy to you, amen.

The Lord is good, a stronghold in the day of trouble;
and He knows those who trust in Him.

Nahum 1:7

I will turn their mourning to joy, will comfort them,
and make them rejoice rather than sorrow.

Jeremiah 31:13

You will show me the path of life; in Your presence is fullness
of joy; at Your right hand are pleasures forevermore.

Psalm 16:11

*Pure and lasting religion in the sight of God
our Father means that we must care for orphans and widows in
their troubles and, refuse to let the world corrupt us.*

THE NAZARETH MANIFESTO

God makes the poor his priority. When the hungry pray, he listens. When orphans cry, he sees.

Jesus, in his first message, declared his passion for the poor. Early in his ministry he returned to his hometown of Nazareth to deliver an inaugural address of sorts. He entered the same synagogue where he had worshipped as a young man and looked into the faces of the villagers. They were simple folk: stonecutters, carpenters, and craftsmen. They survived on minimal wages and lived beneath the shadow of Roman oppression. There wasn't much good news in Nazareth.

But this day was special. Jesus was in town. The hometown boy who had made the big time. They asked him to read Scripture, and he accepted. "And He was handed the book of the prophet Isaiah. And when He had opened the book, He found the place where it was written" (Luke 4:17). . . .

He shuffled the scroll toward the end of the text and read, "The Spirit of the LORD is upon Me, because He has anointed Me to preach the gospel to the poor;

He has sent Me to heal the brokenhearted" (v. 18, quoting Isaiah 61:1).

Jesus lifted his eyes from the parchment and quoted the rest of the words. The crowd, who cherished the words as much as he did, mouthed the lines along with him. "To proclaim liberty to the captives and recovery of sight to the blind, to set at liberty those who are oppressed; to proclaim the acceptable year of the LORD" (vv. 18–19).

Jesus had a target audience. The poor. The brokenhearted. Captives. The blind and oppressed.

His to-do list? Help for the body *and* soul, strength for the physical *and* spiritual, therapy for the temporal *and* eternal. "This is my mission statement," Jesus declared. The Nazareth Manifesto.

–OUTLIVE YOUR LIFE

Precious Lord, you showed us by your life how to be compassionate. You reached out to the poor, the sick, the hurting. You healed their bodies and their souls. You cried over broken hearts, and you smiled when the downtrodden were lifted up. Teach us to do the same. Let our arms reach out to help the oppressed. May we willingly spend our lives serving those in need, amen.

"He has sent Me . . . to set at liberty those who are oppressed."

LUKE 4:18

"I tell you, don't worry about everyday life—whether you have enough."

MATTHEW 6:25 NLT

WORRY DOESN'T WORK

Shortfalls and depletions inhabit our trails. Not enough time, luck, credit, wisdom, intelligence. We are running out of everything, it seems, and so we worry. But worry doesn't work.

> "Look at the birds. They don't need to plant or harvest or put food in barns because your heavenly Father feeds them. And because you are far more valuable to him than they are. Can all your worries add a single moment to your life." (Matthew 6:26–27 NLT)

Fret won't fill a bird's belly with food or a flower's petal with color. Birds and flowers seem to get along just fine, and they don't take antacids.

What's more, you can dedicate a decade of anxious thoughts to the brevity of life and not extend it by one minute. Worry accomplishes nothing. . . .

When legitimate concern morphs into toxic panic, we cross a boundary line into the state of fret. No longer anticipating or preparing, we take up membership in the fraternity of Woe-Be-Me. Christ cautions us against this.

Look at how one translation renders his words: "Therefore I tell you, stop being perpetually uneasy (anxious and worried) about your life" (Matthew 6:25 AMP).

Jesus doesn't condemn legitimate concern for responsibilities but rather the continuous mind-set that dismisses God's presence. Destructive anxiety subtracts God from the future, faces uncertainties with no faith, tallies up the challenges of the day without entering God into the equation. Worry is the darkroom where negatives become glossy prints.

—*FEARLESS*

Father, though you urged us not to worry, we often do just that. We're anxious over things we can't control. We fret about the maybes and what-ifs. Help us remember that you care for the birds, you care about your creatures, and you care about each of your children. When anxious thoughts come to mind, help us turn them over to you. Replace them with calm confidence in you, our loving Father, amen.

And do not seek what you should eat or what you should drink, nor have an anxious mind. For all these things the nations of the world seek after, and your Father knows that you need these things.

LUKE 12:29–30

We love Him because He first loved us.

1 John 4:19

Loved with an Unfailing Love

God loves you with an unfailing love.

England saw a glimpse of such love in 1878. The second daughter of Queen Victoria was Princess Alice. Her young son was infected with a horrible affliction known as black diphtheria. Doctors quarantined the boy and told the mother to stay away.

But she couldn't. One day she overheard him whisper to the nurse, "Why doesn't my mother kiss me anymore?" The words melted her heart. She ran to her son and smothered him with kisses. Within a few days, she was buried.[8]

What would drive a mother to do such a thing? What would lead God to do something greater? Love. Trace the greatest action of God to the greatest attribute of God—his love. . . .

And, oh, what a love this is. It's "too wonderful to be measured" (Ephesians 3:19 CEV). But though we cannot measure it, may I urge you to trust it? Some of you are so hungry for such love. Those who should have loved you didn't. Those who could have loved you wouldn't. You were left at the hospital. Left at the altar. Left with an empty bed. Left with a broken heart. Left with your question, "Does anybody love me?"

Please listen to heaven's answer. As you ponder him on the cross, hear God assure, "I do."

—*It's Not About Me*

Father God, we bring to you our broken hearts and broken dreams. But you reach out to us with the greatest love of all and assure us you will love us forever. Your kind love heals our hurts. Your sacrificial love forgives our sins. May we open our hearts to receive your great love, amen.

May the Lord direct your hearts into the love of God
and into the patience of Christ.

2 Thessalonians 3:5

And we have known and believed the love that God has for us. God is
love, and he who abides in love abides in God, and God in him.

1 John 4:16

Loved with a Perfect Love

If our heart condemns us, God is greater
than our heart, and knows all things.

1 John 3:20

Loved with a Perfect Love

We are convinced that God must hate our evil tendencies. We sure do. We don't like the things we do and say. We despise our lustful thoughts, harsh judgments, and selfish deeds. If our sin nauseates us, how much more must it revolt a holy God! We draw a practical conclusion: God is irreparably ticked off at us. . . .

Yes, we have disappointed God. But, no, God has not abandoned us. . . .

Jesus loves us too much to leave us in doubt about his grace. His "perfect love expels all fear" (1 John 4:18 NLT). If God loved with an imperfect love, we would have high cause to worry. Imperfect love keeps a list of sins and consults it often. God keeps no list of our wrongs. His love casts out fear because he casts out our sin!

Tether your heart to this promise, and tighten the knot. Remember the words of John's epistle: "If our heart condemns us, God is greater than our heart, and knows all things" (1 John 3:20). When you feel unforgiven, evict the feelings. Emotions don't get a vote. Go back to Scripture. God's Word holds rank over self-criticism and self-doubt.

As Paul told Titus, "God's readiness to give and for-give is now public. Salvation's available for everyone! . . . Tell them all this. Build up their courage" (Titus 2:11, 15 MSG). Do you know God's grace? Then you can love boldly, live robustly. You can swing from trapeze to trapeze; his safety net will break your fall.

Nothing fosters courage like a clear grasp of grace.

—*FEARLESS*

Gracious Father, we know that we don't always please you. We fall short of your standards again and again. When we are discouraged and feel we are failing you, remind us of your perfect love and your grace. Thank you for reminding us that your perfect love casts out every wrong and keeps no lists of our failures. Every time we fall, help us to reach for your grace, amen.

[We are] delivered . . . from the power of darkness
and conveyed . . . into the kingdom of the Son.

COLOSSIANS 1:13

"He who believes in Him is not condemned."

JOHN 3:18

The LORD is gracious and full of compassion,
slow to anger and great in mercy.

WHAT MORE DO YOU NEED?

Next time your day goes south, here is what you do. Steep yourself in the grace of God. Saturate your day in his love. Marinate your mind in his mercy. He has settled your accounts, paid your debt. "Christ carried our sins in his body on the cross" (1 Peter 2:24 NCV).

When you lose your temper with your child, Christ intervenes: "I paid for that." When you tell a lie and all of heaven groans, your Savior speaks up: "My death covered that sin." As you lust, gloat, covet, or judge, Jesus stands before the tribunal of heaven and points to the blood-streaked cross. "I've already made provision. I've taken away the sins of the world."

What a gift he has given you. You've won the greatest lottery in the history of humanity, and you didn't even pay for the ticket! Your soul is secure, your salvation guaranteed. Your name is written in the only book that matters. You're only a few sand grains in the hourglass from a tearless, graveless, painless existence. What more do you need?

—*EVERY DAY DESERVES A CHANCE*

Lord, you give gifts without measure. You give the gift of your grace. You give the gift of your mercy. You have settled our debts. You carry our burdens and guide us on the good paths of life. You provide answers and solutions to our problems. You give strength. You have made our souls secure and have promised us life eternal with you. We worship you and seek to bring honor to you, precious Savior, amen.

I will sing to the LORD, because He has dealt bountifully with me.

PSALM 13:6

He will again have compassion on us, and will subdue our iniquities. You will cast all our sins into the depths of the sea.

MICAH 7:19

Though He causes grief, yet He will show compassion according to the multitude of His mercies.

LAMENTATIONS 3:32

He has made His wonderful works to be remembered;
the LORD is gracious and full of compassion.

PSALM 111:4

OUR MESSAGE

"I have a duty to all people," Paul told the Roman church (Romans 1:14 NCV). He had something for them—a message. He'd been entrusted as a Pony Express courier with a divine message, the gospel. Nothing mattered more to Paul than the gospel. "I am not ashamed of the gospel," he wrote next, "because it is the power of God for the salvation of everyone who believes" (v. 16 NIV). . . .

What people think of us matters not. What they think of God matters all. . . .

God doesn't need you and me to do his work. We are expedient messengers, ambassadors by his kindness, not by our cleverness. . . .

And we entrusted with the gospel dare not seek applause but best deflect applause. For our message is about Someone else.

A European village priest in medieval times once gathered his church for a special service. "Come tonight," he told them, "for a special sermon on Jesus." And they did. They came. To their surprise, however, no candles illuminated the sanctuary. They groped their way to the pews and took their seats. The priest was nowhere to be seen. But soon he was heard walking through the church toward the front. When he reached the crucifix that hung on the wall, he lit a candle. Saying nothing, he illuminated the pierced feet of Christ, then the side, then one hand, and then the other. Lifting the candle, he shed light on the blood-masked face and the crown of thorns. With a puff, he blew out the candle and dismissed the church.[9]

May we do nothing more.

May we do nothing less.

–It's Not About Me

Father God, you are the message this world needs to receive. Your loving forgiveness is the antidote for the sins of a world that would be lost without you. Without you there is only pain and hopelessness. With you there is forgiveness, hope, and a future. Let us be your faithful messengers. Help us not to care what others think but to care what you think, amen.

"You are My witnesses," says the LORD, ". . . that you may know and believe Me, and understand that I am He. Before Me there was no God formed, nor shall there be after Me."

ISAIAH 43:10

What do you have that God hasn't given you?
And if all you have is from God, why boast as though
you have accomplished something on your own?

1 Corinthians 4:7 nlt

God Served Us First

The apostle Paul knew to go low and not high. He was saved through a personal visit from Jesus, granted a vision of the heavens and the ability to raise the dead. But when he introduced himself, he simply stated, "I, Paul, am God's slave" (Titus 1:1 msg). John the Baptist was a blood relative of Jesus and one of the most famous evangelists in history. But he is remembered in Scripture as the one who resolved: "He must increase, but I must decrease" (John 3:30). . . .

The greatest example of this humility is none other than Jesus Christ. Who had more reason to boast than he? Yet he never did. He walked on water but never strutted on the beach. He turned a basket into a buffet but never demanded applause. A liberator and a prophet came to visit him, but he never dropped names in his sermon. He could have. "Just the other day I was conferring with Moses and Elijah." But Jesus never thumped his chest. He refused even to take credit. "I can do nothing on my own" (John 5:30 nrsv). He was utterly reliant upon the Father and the Holy Spirit. "All by myself"? Jesus never spoke such words. If he didn't, how dare we?

We can rise too high but can never stoop too low. What gift are you giving that he did not first give? What truth are you teaching that he didn't first teach? You love. But who loved you first? You serve. But who served the most? What are you doing for God that he could not do alone?

How kind of him to use us. How wise of us to remember.

–<small>OUTLIVE YOUR LIFE</small>

Mighty God, we humbly bow before you in thanksgiving for all you have done. Every breath is a gift from you. We cannot do anything without you. Your power and your Word enable us to live each day for you. When we serve, may we serve for your glory. When we love others, may they see your hand, your heart, your love for them, amen.

⌘

The humble He guides in justice, and the humble He teaches His way.

<small>PSALM 25:9</small>

"Blessed are the meek, for they shall inherit the earth."

<small>MATTHEW 5:5</small>

He who has begun a good work in you will complete it until the day of Jesus Christ.

PHILIPPIANS 1:6

A HOPE-FILLED PEOPLE

If you look hard enough and long enough, you'll find something to complain about.

Adam and Eve did. Doesn't the bite into the forbidden fruit reflect a feeling of discontent? Surrounded by all they needed, they set their eyes on the one thing they couldn't have. They found something to complain about.

The followers of Moses did. They could have focused on the miracles: Red Sea becoming the Yellow Brick Road, fire escorting them by night and a cloud accompanying them by day, manna reflecting the morning sunrise and quail scampering into the camp at night. Instead they focused on their problems. They sketched pictures of Egypt, daydreamed of pyramids, and complained that life in the desert wasn't for them. They found something to complain about.

What about you? What are you looking at? The one fruit you can't eat? Or the million you can? The manna or the misery? His plan or your problems? Each a gift or a grind?

Finally, brethren, whatever things are true, whatever things are noble, whatever things are just, whatever things are pure, whatever things are lovely, whatever things are of good report, if there is any virtue and if there is anything praiseworthy—meditate on these things. (Philippians 4:8)

This is more than a silver-lining attitude, more than seeing the cup as half full rather than half empty. This is an admission that unseen favorable forces populate and direct the affairs of humanity. When we see as God wants us to see, we see heaven's hand in the midst of sickness, . . . the Holy Spirit comforting a broken heart. We see not what is seen, but what is unseen. We see with faith and not flesh, and since faith begets hope, we of all people are hope filled. For we know there is more to life than what meets the eye.

–*Every Day Deserves a Chance*

Dear Lord, forgive us when we fail to recognize your hand in our lives. Be patient with us when we focus on our own small plans and fail to see your grand design for our lives. Increase our faith so that we see only your daily love and care, amen.

Happy is he who has the God of Jacob for his help,
whose hope is in the LORD his God.

PSALM 146:5

I have found David the son of Jesse,
a man after My own heart, who will do all My will.

THE HEART GOD LOVES

God called David "a man after my own heart." He gave the appellation to no one else. Not Abraham or Moses or Joseph. He called Paul an apostle, John his beloved, but neither was tagged a man after God's own heart.

One might read David's story and wonder what God saw in him. The fellow fell as often as he stood, stumbled as often as he conquered. He stared down Goliath, yet ogled at Bathsheba; defied God-mockers in the valley, yet joined them in the wilderness. An Eagle Scout one day. Chumming with the Mafia the next. He could lead armies but couldn't manage a family. Raging David. Weeping David. Bloodthirsty. God-hungry. Eight wives. One God.

A man after God's own heart? That God saw him as such gives hope to us all. David's life has little to offer the unstained saint. Straight-A souls find David's story disappointing. The rest of us find it reassuring. We ride the same roller coaster. We alternate between swan dives and belly flops, soufflés and burnt toast.

In David's good moments, no one was better. In his bad moments, could one be worse? The heart God loved was a checkered one.

We need David's story. Some note the absence of miracles in his story. No Red Sea openings, chariots flaming, or dead Lazaruses walking. No miracles.

But there is one. David is one. The God who made a miracle out of David stands ready to make one out of you.

−*Facing Your Giants*

Father, we stand in awe of your wonderful love. A love that sees beyond our sin to significance. A love that patiently forgives. A love that rejoices in our joy and is saddened by our tears. That bears our burdens and lifts our loads. Thank you, Father, for your amazing, miraculous love, amen.

Teach me Your way, O LORD; I will walk in Your truth;
unite my heart to fear Your name.

PSALM 86:11

Cause me to know the way in which I should walk,
for I lift up my soul to You.

PSALM 143:8

"I am with you always, even to the end of the age."
MATTHEW 28:20

"HERE IS GOD"

When ancient sailors sketched maps of the oceans, they disclosed their fears. On the vast unexplored waters, cartographers wrote words such as these:

"Here be dragons."

"Here be demons."

"Here be sirens."

Were a map drawn of your world, would we read such phrases? Over the unknown waters of adulthood, "Here be dragons." Near the sea of the empty nest, "Here be demons." Next to the farthermost latitudes of death and eternity, do we read, "Here be sirens"?

If so, take heart from the example of Sir John Franklin. He was a master mariner in the days of King Henry V. Distant waters were a mystery to him, just as they were to other navigators. Unlike his colleagues, however, Sir John Franklin was a man of faith. The maps that passed through his possession bore the imprimatur of trust. On them he had crossed out the phrases "Here be dragons," "Here be demons," "Here be sirens." In their place he wrote the phrase "Here is God."[10]

Mark it down. You will never go where God is not. You may be transferred, enlisted, commissioned, reassigned, or hospitalized, but—brand this truth on your heart—you can never go where God is not. "I am with you always," Jesus promised (Matthew 28:20).

Don't be afraid; just believe.

—EVERY DAY DESERVES A CHANCE

Father God, you have promised to be with us always. There is no place we can go without your presence. That is why we put our hope in you. Whatever happens, we can rest in your presence and your power. There is only you and your unfailing goodness, amen.

❧

Fear not, for I am with you; be not dismayed, for I am
your God. I will strengthen you, yes, I will help you,
I will uphold you with My righteous right hand.

ISAIAH 41:10

"Peace I leave with you, My peace I give to you; not as the world gives do
I give to you. Let not your heart be troubled, neither let it be afraid."

JOHN 14:27

[God, the Son] loved us and gave himself
up for us as a fragrant offering and sacrifice to God.

THE DEPTHS OF GOD'S LOVE

Who has plumbed the depths of God's love? Only God has. "Want to see the size of my love?" he invites. "Ascend the winding path outside of Jerusalem. Follow the dots of bloody dirt until you crest the hill. Before looking up, pause and hear me whisper, 'This is how much I love you.'"

Whip-ripped muscles drape his back. Blood rivulets cover his face. His eyes and lips are swollen shut. Pain rages at wildfire intensity. As he sinks to relieve the agony of his legs, his airway closes. At the edge of suffocation, he shoves pierced muscles against the spike and inches up the cross. He does this for hours. Painfully up and down until his strength and our doubts are gone.

Does God love you? Behold the cross, and behold your answer.

God the Son died for you. Who could have imagined such a gift? At the time Martin Luther was having his Bible printed in Germany, a printer's daughter encountered God's love. No one had told her about Jesus. Toward God she felt no emotion but fear. One day she gathered pieces of fallen Scripture from the floor. On one paper she found the words "For God so loved the world, that he gave . . ." The rest of the verse had not yet been printed. Still, what she saw was enough to move her. The thought that God would give anything moved her from fear to joy. Her mother noticed the change of attitude. When asked the cause of her happiness, the daughter produced the crumpled piece of partial verse from her pocket. The mother read it and asked, "What did he give?" The child . . . answered, "I do not know. But if He loved us well enough to give us anything, we should not be afraid of Him."[11]

–It's Not About Me

Father, we cannot plumb the depths of your love. For only such an immeasurable love would have sent your Son to suffer for our sins when he himself committed no sin. Because of this we can be restored to a right relationship with you. Thank you for loving us even when we chose not to love you. Thank you for pursuing us patiently with your Holy Spirit. Thank you for making us your children. We cannot fathom such love, but we gratefully accept it, amen.

Neither death nor life, nor angels nor principalities nor powers, nor things present nor things to come, nor height nor depth, nor any other created thing, shall be able to separate us from the love of God.

Romans 8:38–39

Oh, how great is Your goodness, which You have laid up for those who fear You, which You have prepared for those who trust in You.

PSALM 31:19

GOD PROVIDES

Our days stand no chance against the terrorists of the Land of Anxiety. But Christ offers a worry-bazooka. Remember how he taught us to pray? "Give us day by day our daily bread" (Luke 11:3).

This simple sentence unveils God's provision plan: *live one day at a time.* God disclosed the strategy to Moses and the Israelites in the wilderness. "Then the LORD said to Moses, 'Look, I'm going to rain down food from heaven for you. The people can go out each day and pick up as much food as they need for that day'" (Exodus 16:4 NLT).

Note the details of God's provision plan.

He meets daily needs daily. Quail covered the compound in the evenings; manna glistened like fine frost in the mornings. Meat for dinner. Bread for breakfast. The food fell every day. Not annually, monthly, or hourly, but daily. And there is more.

He meets daily needs miraculously. When the people first saw the wafers on the ground, "the Israelites took one look and said to one another, man-hu (What is it?). They had no idea what it was" (v. 15 MSG).

The stunned people named the wafers *man-hu*, Hebrew for "What in the world is this?" God had resources they knew nothing about, solutions outside their reality, provisions outside their possibility. They saw the scorched earth; God saw heaven's breadbasket. They saw dry land; God saw a covey of quail behind every bush. They saw problems; God saw provision.

Anxiety fades as our memory of God's goodness doesn't.

—EVERY DAY DESERVES A CHANCE

Lord, you are a great and good God. You provide for our needs each day. You provide peace when we face problems. You send solutions for our struggles. Your Word guides us with wisdom when we lose our way. May we remember that you carefully measure the events of each day. Today you give us strength for this day, and tomorrow you will give us strength for that day. We depend on you to meet our daily needs each day and in a miraculous way, amen.

In the day when I cried out, You answered me,
and made me bold with strength in my soul.

PSALM 138:3

God is my strength and power, and He makes my way perfect.

2 SAMUEL 22:33

"YES, YOU CAN"

Two types of thoughts continually vie for your attention. One says, "Yes, you can." The other says, "No, you can't." One says, "God will help you." The other lies, "God has left you." . . . One proclaims God's strengths; the other lists your failures. One longs to build you up; the other seeks to tear you down.

And here's the great news: you select the voice you hear. Why listen to the mockers? Why heed their voices? Why give ear to pea brains and scoffers when you can, with the same ear, listen to the voice of God?

Turn a deaf ear to old voices. And, as you do, open your eyes to new choices. . . .

I had a friend who battled the stronghold of alcohol. He tried a fresh tactic. He gave me and a few others permission to slug him in the nose if we ever saw him drinking. . . .

One woman counters her anxiety by memorizing long sections of Scripture. A traveling sales rep asks hotels to remove the television from his room so he won't be tempted to watch adult movies. Another man grew so weary of his prejudice that he moved into a minority neighborhood, made new friends, and changed his attitude.

Turn a deaf ear to the old voices.

Open a wide eye to the new choices.

–*Facing Your Giants*

Lord, your word has promised that we can do all things through you because you give us strength. Our hope is in you, Father. Teach us to concentrate on your strengths rather than on our failures. Grant us grace to do our part in overcoming difficulties, and give us the wisdom to know when to let you do your part, amen.

Holding fast the word of life, so that I may rejoice in the day of Christ that I have not run in vain or labored in vain.

PHILIPPIANS 2:16

"These things I have spoken to you, that in Me you may have peace. In the world you will have tribulation; but be of good cheer, I have overcome the world."

JOHN 16:33

When He saw the multitudes, He was moved with compassion for them,
because they were weary and scattered, like sheep having no shepherd.

MATTHEW 9:36

LET'S HURT WITH THE HURTING

What do we see when we see . . .

- the figures beneath the overpass, encircling the fire in a five-gallon drum?
- the news clips of children in refugee camps?

What do we see? "When [Jesus] saw the multitudes, He was moved with compassion for them, because they were weary and scattered, like sheep having no shepherd" (Matthew 9:36). . . .

Let's be the people who look at the hurting until we hurt with them. No hurrying past, turning away, or shifting of eyes. No pretending or glossing over. Let's look at the face until we see the person.

A family in our congregation lives with the heartbreaking reality that their son is homeless. He ran away when he was seventeen, and with the exception of a few calls from prison and one visit, they have had no contact with him for twenty years. The mom allowed me to interview her at a leadership gathering. As we prepared for the discussion, I asked her why she was willing to disclose her story.

"I want to change the way people see the homeless. I want them to stop seeing problems and begin seeing mothers' sons."

Change begins with a genuine look. And continues with a helping hand.

Works done in God's name long outlive our earthly lives.

—OUTLIVE YOUR LIFE

Lord, we are surrounded by hurting people who have no hope. They are miserable and lost without your mercy. Forgive us when we turn away from them in careless indifference. May our hearts be broken with the things that break your heart. May we look into the face of every hurting person and extend a helping hand. Teach us to touch desperate lives with works done in your name. Soften our hearts to love others as freely and graciously as you have loved us. Let us be your hand extended, amen.

But concerning brotherly love you have no need that I should write to you, for you yourselves are taught by God to love one another.

1 THESSALONIANS 4:9

"Greater love has no one than this,
than to lay down one's life for his friends."

JOHN 15:13

"This is the will of Him who sent Me, that everyone who sees the Son and believes in Him may have everlasting life."

OUR PART IS TO TRUST

It's a simple promise. . . . "Everyone who believes in [him] will have eternal life" (John 3:15 NLT).

The simplicity troubles many people. We expect a more complicated cure, a more elaborate treatment. . . . We expect a more proactive assignment, to have to conjure up a remedy for our sin. Some mercy seekers have donned hair shirts, climbed cathedral steps on their knees, or traversed hot rocks on bare feet.

Others of us have written our own Bible verse: "God helps those who help themselves" (Popular Opinion 1:1). We'll fix ourselves, thank you. We'll make up for our mistakes with contributions, our guilt with busyness. We'll overcome failures with hard work. We'll find salvation the old-fashioned way: we'll earn it.

Christ, in contrast, says: "Your part is to trust. Trust me to do what you can't."

By the way, you take similar steps of trust daily, even hourly. You believe the chair will support you, so you set your weight on it. You believe water will hydrate you, so you swallow it. You trust the work of the light switch, so you flip it. You have faith the doorknob will work, so you turn it.

You regularly trust power you cannot see to do a work you cannot accomplish. Jesus invites you to do the same with him.

Just him. Not . . . any other leader. . . . Not even you. You can't fix you. Look to Jesus . . . and believe.

–3:16: The Numbers of Hope

Lord, you have invited us to trust you for salvation and for everything we need. You've promised rest and restoration if we will simply trust in you. Teach us to trust you more. Forgive us when we struggle to do what you long to do for us, amen.

But God, who is rich in mercy, because of His great love
with which He loved us, even when we were dead
in trespasses, made us alive together with Christ.

Ephesians 2:4–5

His divine power has given to us all things
that pertain to life and godliness, through the knowledge
of Him who called us by glory and virtue.

2 Peter 1:3

In all your ways acknowledge Him, and He shall direct your paths.
PROVERBS 3:6

PRAYER IS THIS SIMPLE

My father let me climb onto his lap . . . when he drove! He'd be arrested for doing so today. But half a century ago, no one cared. Especially on a flat-as-a-skillet West Texas oil field, where rabbits outnumber people. . . .

I loved it. Did it matter that I couldn't see over the dash? That my feet stopped two feet shy of the brake and accelerator? That I didn't know a radio from a carburetor? By no means. I helped my dad drive his truck.

Did I fear driving into the ditch? Overturning the curve? Running the tire into a rut? By no means. Dad's hands were next to mine, his eyes keener than mine. Consequently, I was fearless! Anyone can drive a car from the lap of a father.

And anyone can pray from the same perspective.

Prayer is the practice of sitting calmly in God's lap and placing our hands on his steering wheel. He handles the speed and hard curves and ensures safe arrival. And we offer our requests; we ask God to "take this cup away." (Mark 14:36) This cup of disease, betrayal, financial collapse, joblessness, conflict, or senility. Prayer is this simple.

Be specific about your fears. . . . Putting your worries into words disrobes them. They look silly standing there naked.

—*FEARLESS*

Thank you, gracious God, for the privilege of prayer. How amazing that we can talk to you anywhere, anytime. What a relief to share our burdens and blessings with you, dear Father. What a delight to know that you hear and answer every prayer, amen.

"Whatever you ask in My name, that I will do,
that the Father may be glorified in the Son."

JOHN 14:13

I prayed, and the LORD has granted me
my petition which I asked of Him.

1 SAMUEL 1:27

I sought the LORD, and He heard me,
and delivered me from all my fears.

PSALM 34:4

He knows our frame; He remembers that we are dust.

PSALM 103:14

ENDLESS JOY

The brevity of life grants power to abide, not an excuse to bail. Fleeting days don't justify fleeing problems. Fleeting days strengthen us to endure problems. Will your problems pass? No guarantee they will. Will your pain cease? Perhaps. Perhaps not. But heaven gives this promise: "Our light affliction, which is but for a moment, is working for us a far more exceeding and eternal weight of glory" (2 Corinthians 4:17).

The words "weight of glory" conjure up images of the ancient pan scale. Remember the blindfolded lady of justice? She holds a pan scale—two pans, one on either side of the needle. The weight of a purchase would be determined by placing weights on one side and the purchase on the other.

God does the same with your struggles. On one side he stacks all your burdens. Famines. Firings. Parents who forgot you. Bosses who ignored you. Bad breaks, bad health, bad days. Stack them up, and watch one side of the pan scale plummet.

Now witness God's response. Does he remove them? Eliminate the burdens? No, rather than take them, he offsets them. He places an eternal weight of glory on the other side. Endless joy. Measureless peace. An eternity of him.

–*It's Not About Me*

Heavenly Father, you have promised us an eternity of endless joy with you. Knowing this encourages us to stand firm during the difficult times of life. We know that you are balancing our suffering with an eternal weight of glory. May our response to testing in this life bring glory to your name now and through all eternity. Give us the strength and courage to endure faithfully our struggles through your grace and mercy, amen.

Yet I will rejoice in the LORD, I will joy in the God of my salvation.

HABAKKUK 3:18

My soul shall be joyful in the LORD; it shall rejoice in His salvation.

PSALM 35:9

I will greatly rejoice in the LORD, my soul shall be joyful in my God; for He has clothed me with the garments of salvation, He has covered me with the robe of righteousness.

ISAIAH 61:10

The eyes of the LORD are on the righteous,
and His ears are open to their prayers.

1 PETER 3:12

LET'S TALK TO JESUS

What do you do when you run out of gas? You don't exhaust your petroleum perhaps, but all of us run out of something. You need kindness, but the gauge is on empty. You need hope, but the needle is in the red. You want five gallons of solutions but can only muster a few drops. When you run out of steam before you run out of day, what do you do? Stare at the gauge? Blame your upbringing? Deny the problem?

No. Pity won't start the car. Complaints don't fuel an engine. Denial doesn't bump the needle. In the case of an empty tank, we've learned: get the car to a gas pump ASAP.

My first thought when I run out of fuel is, *How can I get this car to a gas pump?* Your first thought when you have a problem should be, *How can I get this problem to Jesus?*

Let's get practical. You and your spouse are about to battle it out again. The thunderstorm looms on the horizon. The temperature is dropping, and lightning bolts are flashing. Both of you need patience, but both tanks are empty. What if one of you calls, "Time-out"? What if one of you says, "Let's talk to Jesus before we talk to each other. In fact, let's talk to Jesus until we can talk to each other"? Couldn't hurt. After all, he broke down the walls of Jericho. Perhaps he could do the same for yours.

–EVERY DAY DESERVES A CHANCE

Lord, you are the answer to our questions and the solution to our problems. We don't have the wisdom to work through the storms of life, but you do. In your presence we find help and hope and healing, amen.

Thus says the LORD, the God of David. . . . :
"I have heard your prayer, I have seen your tears."

ISAIAH 38:5

I love the LORD, because He has heard my voice and my supplications.

PSALM 116:1

They cried out to the LORD in their trouble,
and He saved them out of their distresses.

PSALM 107:19

The world is passing away, and the lust of it;
but he who does the will of God abides forever.

1 John 2:17

Heaven Is a Perfect Place

In heaven you will be you at your best forever. Even now you have your good moments. Occasional glimpses of your heavenly self. When you change your baby's diaper, forgive your boss's temper, tolerate your spouse's moodiness, you display traces of saintliness. It's the other moments that sour life. Tongue, sharp as a razor. Moods as unpredictable as Mount Saint Helens. This part wearies you.

But God impounds imperfections at his gate. His light silences the wolf man within. "Nothing that is impure will enter the city" (Revelation 21:27 TEV). Pause and let this promise drench you. Can you envision your sinless existence?

You will be you at your best forever!

And you'll enjoy everyone else at their prime! As it is, one of us is always a step behind. Bad moods infect the best of families. Complaints shadow the clearest days. Bad apples spoil bunches of us, but rotten fruit doesn't qualify for the produce section of heaven. Christ will have completed his redemptive work. All gossip excised and jealousy extracted. He will suction the last drop of orneriness from the most remote corners of our souls. You'll love the result. No one will doubt your word, question your motives, or speak evil behind your back. God's sin purging discontinues all strife.

Heaven is a perfect place of perfected people with our perfect Lord. "Oh, the depth of the riches both of the wisdom and knowledge of God! How unsearchable are His judgments and His ways past finding out!" (Romans 11:33).

–3:16: THE NUMBERS OF HOPE

Loving Father, what a precious day it will be when we stand in your presence, perfect and whole. What relief it will be to finally be just like Jesus. Thank you for preparing a heavenly home for us, and thank you for preparing us for that heavenly home. Father, we want to please you and know that on the day we stand before your throne, you will have purged all the sin from our lives. What a glorious day that will be! Amen.

I know that whatever God does, it shall be forever.
Nothing can be added to it, and nothing taken from it.

ECCLESIASTES 3:14

Blessed be the God and Father of our Lord Jesus Christ, who has blessed us with every spiritual blessing in the heavenly places in Christ.

EPHESIANS 1:3

God made Christ, who never sinned, to be the offering for our sin,
so that we could be made right with God through Christ.

2 CORINTHIANS 5:21 NLT

THE BREAD OF LIFE

Would you consider the offer of Jesus? "I am the bread of life. No one who comes to me will ever be hungry again" (John 6:35 NLT).

The grain-to-bread process is a demanding one. The seed must be planted before it can grow. When the grain is ripe, it must be cut down and ground into flour. Before it can become bread, it must pass through the oven. Bread is the end result of planting, harvesting, and heating.

Jesus endured an identical process. He was born into this world. He was cut down, bruised, and beaten on the threshing floor of Calvary. He passed through the fire of God's wrath, for our sake. He "suffered because of others' sins, the Righteous One for the unrighteous ones. He went through it all—was put to death and then made alive—to bring us to God" (1 Peter 3:18 MSG).

Bread of Life? Jesus lived up to the title. But an unopened loaf does a person no good. Have you received the bread? Have you received God's forgiveness? . . .

God does not give us what we deserve. He has drenched his world in grace. It has no end. It knows no limits. It empowers this life and enables us to live the next. God offers second chances, like a soup kitchen offers meals to everyone who asks.

And that includes you. Make sure you reccive the bread.

–OUTLIVE YOUR LIFE

Dear Lord, thank you for being the bread of life. You offer to us the sustenance we need for our spiritual lives. As bread feeds our physical bodies, so your Word and your wisdom provide food for our spirits. Your gift of salvation brings us to God and enables us to live for him. You offer this gift freely to all who will accept it. We gladly receive this bread of life, and we praise you for drenching this world in grace and giving us what we did not deserve, amen.

"I am the living bread which came down from heaven. If anyone eats of this bread, he will live forever; and the bread that I shall give is My flesh which I shall give for the life of the world."

JOHN 6:51

*Not to us, O LORD, . . . but to Your name give glory
because of your lovingkindness, because of Your truth.*

PSALM 115:1 NASB

GOD CAN RESCUE US

God has one goal: God. "I have my reputation to keep up" (Isaiah 48:11 MSG).

Surprised? Isn't such an attitude, dare we ask, self-centered? Don't we deem this behavior "self-promotion"? Why does God broadcast himself?

For the same reason the pilot of the lifeboat does. Think of it this way. You're floundering neck-deep in a dark, cold sea. Ship sinking. Life jacket deflating. Strength waning. Through the inky night comes the voice of a lifeboat pilot. But you cannot see him. What do you want the driver of the lifeboat to do?

Be quiet? Say nothing? Stealth his way through the drowning passengers? By no means! You need volume! Amp it up, buddy! In biblical jargon, you want him to show his glory. You need to hear him say, "I am here. I am strong. I have room for you. I can save you!" Drowning passengers want the pilot to reveal his preeminence.

Don't we want God to do the same? Look around. People thrash about in seas of guilt, anger, despair. Life isn't working. We are going down fast. But God can rescue us. And only one message matters. His! We need to see God's glory.

Make no mistake. God has no ego problem. *He does not reveal his glory for his good. We need to witness it for ours.* We need a strong hand to pull us into a safe boat. And once aboard, what becomes our priority?

Simple. Promote God. We declare his preeminence. "Hey! Strong boat over here! Able pilot! He can pull you out!"

–It's Not About Me

Father God, we gladly choose to make you the priority in our lives. We want to make you and your message preeminent. We are grateful that you reached out through the fog of life with your saving message and gave us the opportunity to let you pull us to safety. The salvation you offer is the safety net of life and we gladly accept your offer. May we be eager to tell others of your saving love. May we promote your glory so others will find safety in you, amen.

Sing about the glory of his name!
Tell the world how glorious he is.

Psalm 66:2 nlt

"Most assuredly, I say to you, unless one is born of water and the Spirit, he cannot enter the kingdom of God."

JOHN 3:5

GOD RESTORES THE BEAUTY

Born again. Birth, by definition, is a passive act. The enwombed child contributes nothing to the delivery. Postpartum celebrations applaud the work of the mother. No one lionizes the infant. ("Great work there, little one.") No, give the tyke a pacifier not a medal. Mom deserves the gold. She exerts the effort. She pushes, agonizes, and delivers.

When my niece bore her first child, she invited her brother and mother to stand in the delivery room. After witnessing three hours of pushing, when the baby finally crowned, my nephew turned to his mom and said, "I'm sorry for every time I talked back to you."

The mother pays the price of birth. She doesn't enlist the child's assistance or solicit his or her advice. Why would she? The baby can't even take a breath without umbilical help, much less navigate a path into new life. Nor, Jesus is saying, can we. Spiritual rebirthing requires a capable parent, not an able infant.

Who is this parent? . . .

He who did it first must do it again. The original creator re-creates his creation. This is the act Jesus describes.

Born: God exerts the effort.

Again: God restores the beauty.

We don't *try* again. We need not the muscle of self, but a miracle of God.

—3:16: THE NUMBERS OF HOPE

Almighty God, your gift of salvation is a miraculous gift, the death of your Son, Jesus Christ. There is nothing we could do to deserve this amazing gift. Thank you for giving it freely to all who will accept it. We praise you for providing the path to a new life for your children. How blessed are those who have you living in their hearts, amen.

In Him we have redemption through His blood,
the forgiveness of sins, according to the riches of His grace which
He made to abound toward us in all wisdom and prudence.

EPHESIANS 1:7–8

"When everything is ready, I will come and get you,
so that you will always be with me where I am."
JOHN 14:3 NLT

IT'S NOT AN EMPTY PROMISE

This is the promise of Christ: "Don't let your hearts be troubled. You trust God, now trust in me. There are many rooms in my Father's home. . . . If this were not so, I would tell you plainly. When everything is ready, I will come and get you, so that you will always be with me where I am" (John 14:1–3 NLT). . . .

He promised not just an afterlife, but a better life.

"There are many rooms in my Father's home, and I am going to prepare a place for you." We Westerners might miss the wedding images, but . . . Jesus' listeners didn't. This was a groom-to-bride promise. Upon receiving the permission of both families, the groom returned to the home of his father and built a home for his bride. He "prepared a place."

By promising to do the same for us, Jesus elevates funerals to the same hope level as weddings. From his perspective the trip to the cemetery and the walk down the aisle warrant identical excitement. . . .

Both celebrate a new era, name, and home. In both, the groom walks the bride away on his arm. Jesus is your coming groom. "I will come and get you. . . ." He will meet you at the altar. Your final glimpse of life will trigger your first glimpse of him.

But how can we be sure he will keep this pledge? Do we have any guarantee that his words are more than empty poetry or vain superstition? Dare we set our hope and hearts in the hands of a small-town Jewish carpenter? The answer rests in the Jerusalem graveyard. If Jesus' tomb is empty, then his promise is not.

—*FEARLESS*

Father, you have given us so many precious promises. One of the most blessed is the promise that you are preparing a heavenly home for your children. When we face our final days on earth, we can rest assured that you will keep your pledge to take us home. We set our hopes and hearts on you, Lord. It will be not just an afterlife, but a better life, amen.

And they will see the Son of Man coming on the clouds of heaven with power and great glory. And He will send His angels with a great sound of a trumpet, and they will gather together His elect from the four winds, from one end of heaven to the other.

MATTHEW 24:30–31

To whom then will you liken God?
Or what likeness will you compare with Him?

ISAIAH 40:18 NASB

HE IS GOD ALONE

To what can we compare God? "Who in the skies is comparable to the LORD? Who among the sons of the mighty is like the LORD?" (Psalm 89:6 NASB).

Any pursuit of God's counterpart is vain. Any search for a godlike person or position on earth is futile. No one and nothing compares with him. No one advises him. No one helps him. It is he who "executes judgment, putting down one and lifting up another" (Psalm 75:7 ESV).

You and I may have power. But God *is* power. We may be a lightning bug, but he is lightning itself. "Wisdom and power are his" (Daniel 2:20 NIV).

Consider the universe around us. Unlike the potter who takes something and reshapes it, God took nothing and created something. God created everything that exists by divine fiat *ex nihilo* (out of nothing). He did not rely on material that was preexistent or coeternal. Prior to creation, the universe was not a dark space. The universe did not exist. God even created the darkness. "I am the one who creates the light and makes the darkness" (Isaiah 45:7 NLT). John proclaimed, "You created everything, and it is for your pleasure that they exist and were created" (Revelation 4:11 NLT). . . .

Even God asks, "To whom will you compare me? Who is my equal?" (Isaiah 40:25 NLT). As if his question needed an answer, he gives one: "I am God—I alone! I am God, and there is no one else like me" (46:9 NLT).

–*It's Not About Me*

Lord God, there is no one like you. You are beyond compare. You alone are God. You alone are mighty and powerful. All wisdom belongs to you. The world exists as your amazing creation. We are blessed to be your children. Our minds can hardly comprehend that you, holy Lord God, love us and care about the smallest details of our lives. We can only stand humbly before you and praise your glorious name, amen.

You are worthy, O Lord, to receive glory and honor and power; for You created all things, and by Your will they exist and were created.

REVELATION 4:11

Blessed be the name of God forever and ever,
for wisdom and might are His.

DANIEL 2:20

*"Do not worry about tomorrow, for tomorrow will worry about its
own things. Sufficient for the day is its own trouble."*

MATTHEW 6:34

FACE CHALLENGES IN STAGES

An accomplished Ironman triathlete told me the secret of his success. "You last the long race by running short ones." Don't swim 2.4 miles; just swim to the next buoy. Rather than bike 112 miles, ride 10, take a break, and bike 10 more. Never tackle more than the challenge ahead.

Didn't Jesus offer the same counsel? "So don't ever worry about tomorrow. After all, tomorrow will worry about itself. Each day has enough trouble of its own" (Matthew 6:34 GOD'S WORD).

When asked how he managed to write so many books, Joel Henderson explained that he'd never written a book. All he did was write one page a day.[12]

Face challenges in stages. You can't control your temper forever, but you can control it for the next hour. Earning a college degree can seem impossible, but studying one semester is manageable, and logging in one good week is doable. You last the long race by running the short ones.

—*EVERY DAY DESERVES A CHANCE*

Lord, you taught us how to face our challenges when you told us to live one day at a time. Each day brings its own perplexing problems. You remind us that we don't need to borrow worry from tomorrow. Help us to face daily demands each day by living in your love moment by moment and hour by hour. You have promised to be with us and to lead and guide us. We take each step of life and breathe each breath of life under your watchful care. Forgive us when we fret about the future. Help us to rest continually in you, amen.

In Your hand is power and might; in Your hand
it is to make great and to give strength to all.

1 CHRONICLES 29:12

Let the peace of God rule in your hearts,
to which also you were called in one body; and be thankful.

COLOSSIANS 3:15

I will call upon the LORD, who is worthy to be praised;
so shall I be saved from my enemies.

2 SAMUEL 22:4

You will keep him in perfect peace,
whose mind is stayed on You, because he trusts in You.

ISAIAH 26:3

FIX YOUR THOUGHTS ON GOD

Goliaths still roam our world. Debt. Disaster. Dialysis. Danger. Deceit. Disease. Depression. Supersize challenges still swagger and strut, still pilfer sleep and embezzle peace and liposuction joy. But they can't dominate you. You know how to deal with them. You face giants by facing God first.

Don't face your giant without first dedicating time to prayer. Paul, the apostle, wrote, "Prayer is essential in this ongoing warfare. Pray hard and long" (Ephesians 6:18 MSG).

Prayer spawned David's successes. His Brook Besor wisdom grew out of the moment he "strengthened himself in the LORD his God" (1 Samuel 30:6). When Saul's soldiers tried to capture him, David turned toward God: "You have been my defense and refuge in the day of my trouble" (Psalm 59:16).

How do you survive a fugitive life in the caves? David did with prayers like this one: "Be good to me, God—and now! I've run to you for dear life. I'm hiding out under your wings until the hurricane blows over. I call out to High God, the God who holds me together" (57:1–2 MSG).

When David soaked his mind in God, he stood. When he didn't, he flopped. You think he spent much time in prayer the evening he seduced Bathsheba? Did he write a psalm the day he murdered Uriah? Doubtful.

Mark well this promise: "[God] will keep in perfect peace all who trust in [God], whose thoughts are fixed on [God]!" (Isaiah 26:3 NLT). God promises not just peace, but perfect peace. Undiluted, unspotted, unhindered peace. To whom? To those whose minds are "fixed" on God. Forget occasional glances. Dismiss random ponderings. Peace is promised to the one who fixes thoughts and desires on the king.

–FACING YOUR GIANTS

Father God, you have promised peace of mind to those who fix their thoughts on you. You have shown us how to deal with the "giants" we encounter so they won't dominate our lives. Like David of old, may we soak our minds in you, Lord, and run straight to you with our problems. Teach us to make prayer the highest priority. Remind us of your promises to hear and answer our prayers, amen.

You shall love the LORD . . . with all your mind.

MARK 12:30

These little troubles are getting us ready for an eternal glory
that will make all our troubles seem like nothing.

2 Corinthians 4:17 cev

Keep an Eternal Perspective

What about the tragic changes God permits? . . . Who can find a place in life's puzzle for the deformity of a child or the enormity of an earthquake's devastation? When a company discontinues a position or a parent is deployed . . . do such moments serve a purpose?

They do if we see them from an eternal perspective. What makes no sense in this life will make perfect sense in the next. I have proof: you in the womb.

I know you don't remember this prenatal season, so let me remind you what happened during it. Every gestation day equipped you for your earthly life. Your bones solidified, your eyes developed, the umbilical cord transported nutrients into your growing frame . . . for what reason? So you might remain enwombed? Quite the contrary. Womb time equipped you for earth time, suited you up for your postpartum existence.

Some prenatal features went unused before birth. You grew a nose but didn't breathe. Eyes developed, but could you see? Your tongue, toenails, and crop of hair served no function in your mother's belly. But aren't you glad you have them now?

Certain chapters in this life seem so unnecessary, like nostrils on the preborn. Suffering. Loneliness. Disease. Holocausts. Martyrdom. Monsoons. If we assume this world exists just for pregrave happiness, these atrocities disqualify it from doing so. But what if this earth is the womb? Might these challenges, severe as they may be, serve to prepare us, equip us for the world to come? As Paul wrote, "These little troubles are *getting us ready* for an eternal glory that will make all our troubles seem like nothing" (2 Corinthians 4:17 CEV).

—*FEARLESS*

Heavenly Father, we don't have to look far to find tragic events in this world. They are prevalent and puzzling and perplexing. They don't make sense, and they fill our hearts with sorrow. Help us look at these events from an eternal perspective. Remind us that even tragic events serve your purpose. Use our troubles and trials to shape us for a heavenly life with you, amen.

Dear friends, do not be surprised at the painful trial you are suffering, as though something strange were happening to you. But rejoice that you participate in the sufferings of Christ, so that you may be overjoyed when his glory is revealed.

1 PETER 4:12–13

Casting all your care upon Him, for He cares for you.

1 PETER 5:7

P-E-A-C-E-F-U-L

Here are eight worry stoppers:

1. *Pray, first.* Don't pace up and down the floors of the waiting room; pray for a successful surgery. Don't bemoan the collapse of an investment; ask God to help you. . . .
2. *Easy, now.* Slow down. . . . Assess the problem. Take it to Jesus and state it clearly.
3. *Act on it.* Become a worry-slapper. Treat frets like mosquitoes. . . . The moment a concern surfaces, deal with it. Don't dwell on it. Head off worries before they get the best of you. . . .
4. *Compile a worry list.* Over a period of days, record your anxious thoughts. Maintain a list of all the things that trouble you. Then review them. How many of them turned into a reality? . . .
5. *Evaluate your worry categories.* Your list will highlight themes of worry. You'll detect recurring areas of preoccupation. . . . Pray specifically about them.
6. *Focus on today.* God meets daily needs daily. Not weekly or annually. He will give you what you need when it is needed.

7. *Unleash a worry army*. Share your feelings with a few loved ones. Ask them to pray with and for you.
8. *Let God be enough*. Seek first the kingdom of wealth, and you'll worry over every dollar. Seek first the kingdom of health, and you'll sweat every blemish and bump. . . . But seek first his kingdom, and you will find it. On that, we can depend and never worry.

Eight steps. Pray, first. Easy, now. Act on it. Compile a worry list. Evaluate your worry categories. Focus on today. Unleash a worry army. Let God be enough. P-E-A-C-E-F-U-L.

—*Fearless*

Father God, thank you for pouring peace in our lives. When all around us tries to steal our tranquillity, trusting you takes us back to peace. You've promised that when we seek you, we will find you. And when we find you, we will find rest for our spirits. Thank you, Lord, for caring about the things that trouble us and try to take our peace. Thank you for being a fountain of comfort, amen.

You did not receive the spirit of bondage again to fear, but you received the Spirit of adoption by whom we cry out, "Abba, Father."

Romans 8:15

The LORD spoke to Moses face to face, as a man speaks to his friend.
EXODUS 33:11

LOVED BY A GLORIOUS GOD

Moses makes a request of God. "Show me your glory" (Exodus 33:18 NCV).

"Show me your radiance," Moses is praying. "Flex your biceps. Let me see the *S* on your chest. Your preeminence. Your heart-stopping, ground-shaking extraspectacularness. Forget the money and the power. Bypass the youth. I can live with an aging body, but I can't live without you. I want more God, please. I'd like to see more of your glory."

Why did Moses want to see God's greatness?

Ask yourself a similar question. Why do you stare at sunsets and ponder the summer night sky? Why do you search for a rainbow in the mist or gaze at the Grand Canyon? Why do you allow the Pacific surf to mesmerize and Niagara to hypnotize? How do we explain our fascination with such sights?

Beauty? Yes. But doesn't the beauty point to a beautiful Someone? Doesn't the immensity of the ocean suggest an immense Creator? Doesn't the rhythm of migrating cranes and beluga whales hint of a brilliant mind? And isn't that what we desire? A beautiful Maker?

An immense Creator? A God so mighty that he can commission the birds and command the fish?

"Show me your glory, God," Moses begs. . . .

We cross a line when we make such a request. When our deepest desire is not the things of God, or a favor from God, but God himself, we cross a threshold. Less self-focus, more God-focus. Less about me, more about him.

–*It's Not About Me*

Gracious Lord, like Moses of old we long to see your greatness and your glory. When we see the wonders of your creation, our hearts are filled with praise for your mighty power. You care for even the smallest detail of creation. Your vast universe is spectacular beyond imagining. We want to know you better, Lord, amen.

Be exalted, O God, above the heavens,
and Your glory above all the earth.

PSALM 108:5

Unto You I lift up my eyes, O You who dwell in the heavens.

PSALM 123:1

> *"Come to Me, all you who labor and are*
> *heavy laden, and I will give you rest."*
> MATTHEW 11:28

THE SOLUTION FOR SLUMPS

Slumps: the petri dish for bad decisions, the incubator for wrong turns, the assembly line of regretful moves. How we handle our tough times stays with us for a long time.

How do you handle yours? When hope takes the last train and joy is nothing but the name of the girl down the street . . . when you are tired of trying, tired of forgiving, tired of hard weeks or hardheaded people . . . how do you manage your dark days?

With a bottle of pills or scotch? With an hour at the bar, a day at the spa, or a week at the coast? Many opt for such treatments. So many, in fact, that we assume they reenergize the sad life. But do they? No one denies that they help for a while, but over the long haul? They numb the pain, but do they remove it?

Or are we like the sheep on the Turkish cliff? Who knows why the first one jumped over the edge. Even more bizarre are the fifteen hundred others who followed, each leaping off the same overhang.

The first 450 animals died. The thousand that followed survived only because the pile of corpses cushioned their fall.[13]

We, like sheep, follow each other over the edge, falling headlong into bars and binges and beds. . . .

Is there a solution? Indeed there is: . . . *be quick to pray*. Stop talking to yourself. Talk to Christ, who invites. "Are you tired? Worn out? Burned out on religion? Come to me. Get away with me and you'll recover your life. I'll show you how to take a real rest" (Matthew 11:28 MSG).

God, who is never downcast, never tires of your down days.

–*Facing Your Giants*

Father, when we find ourselves sinking from the weight of earthly distractions, you have promised to help us find a solution. When days are dark, you long to bring light to our lives. Thank you for never getting tired of lifting us up on down days. Teach us to turn to you in prayer when we're overwhelmed with discouraging thoughts. Guide us in your word when we feel lost and alone. In your presence we will find joy, amen.

Why are you cast down, O my soul? And why are you disquieted within me? Hope in God; for I shall yet praise Him.

Psalm 43:5

*"Do not fear, little flock, for it is your Father's
good pleasure to give you the kingdom."*

LUKE 12:32

LIVING WITHOUT FEAR

Fear feels dreadful. It sucks the life out of the soul, curls
us into an embryonic state, and drains us dry of content-
ment. We become abandoned barns, rickety and tilting
from the winds, a place where humanity used to eat,
thrive, and find warmth. No longer. When fear shapes
our lives, safety becomes our god. When safety becomes
our god, we worship the risk-free life. Can the safety lover
do anything great? Can the risk-averse accomplish noble
deeds? For God? For others? No. The fear-filled cannot
love deeply. Love is risky. They cannot give to the poor.
Benevolence has no guarantee of return. The fear-filled
cannot dream wildly. What if their dreams sputter and
fall from the sky? The worship of safety emasculates
greatness. No wonder Jesus wages such a war against fear.

His most common command emerges from the
"fear not" genre. The gospels list some 125 Christ-issued
imperatives. Of these, twenty-one urge us to "not be
afraid" or "not fear" or "have courage" or "take heart" or
"be of good cheer." The second most common command, to love God and neighbor, appears on only eight
occasions. If quantity is any indicator, Jesus takes our

fears seriously. The one statement he made more than any other was this: don't be afraid.

—*FEARLESS*

O Lord, you are constantly calling us to be courageous and to trust completely in you. But too often fear gets the upper hand. Give us your peace when we edge toward panic. May we focus on you when our faith is fragile. Help us to remember that you want our lives to be filled with hope and gladness. Remind us of your loving care and compassion that covers every detail of our lives, amen.

The LORD, He is the one who goes before you. He will be with you, He will not leave you nor forsake you; do not fear nor be dismayed.

DEUTERONOMY 31:8

Be of good courage, and He shall strengthen your heart, all you who hope in the LORD.

PSALM 31:24

"If any of you want to be my followers, you must forget about yourself. You must take up your cross each day and follow me."
LUKE 9:23 CEV

FILL YOUR DAY WITH G-O-D

My friend and I went on an extended hill-country trek. A few minutes into the trip I began to tire. Within a half hour my thighs ached and my lungs heaved like a beached whale. I could scarcely pump the pedals. I'm no Tour de France contender, but neither am I a newcomer, yet I felt like one. After forty-five minutes I had to dismount and catch my breath. That's when my partner spotted the problem. Both rear brakes were rubbing my back tire! Rubber grips contested every pedal stroke. The ride was destined to be a tough one.

Don't we do the same? Guilt presses on one side. Dread drags the other. No wonder we weary so. We sabotage our day, wiring it for disaster, lugging along yesterday's troubles, downloading tomorrow's struggles. Remorse over the past, anxiety over the future. We aren't giving the day a chance.

How can we? What can we do? Here's my proposal: consult Jesus. The Ancient of Days has something to say about our days. He doesn't use the term *day* very often in Scripture. But the few times he does use it provide a delightful formula for upgrading each of ours to blue-ribbon status.

Saturate your day in his grace.

"I tell you in solemn truth," replied Jesus, "that this very day you shall be with me in Paradise" (Luke 23:43 WEY).

Entrust your day to his oversight.

"Give us day by day our daily bread" (Luke 11:3).

Accept his direction.

"If any of you want to be my followers, you must forget about yourself. You must take up your cross each day and follow me" (Luke 9:23 CEV).

Grace. Oversight. Direction. G-O-D

Fill your day with God. Give the day a chance.

—*EVERY DAY DESERVES A CHANCE*

Father God, we want to fill our days with you. Help us saturate our days with your grace. We entrust our days to your oversight and accept your direction. You have promised to give us exactly what we need for each day, and we thank you for that provision. And you have promised to be the light we need on the path. You are the way and the truth for our path, amen.

My tongue will speak of your righteousness
and of your praises all day long.

PSALM 35:28 NIV

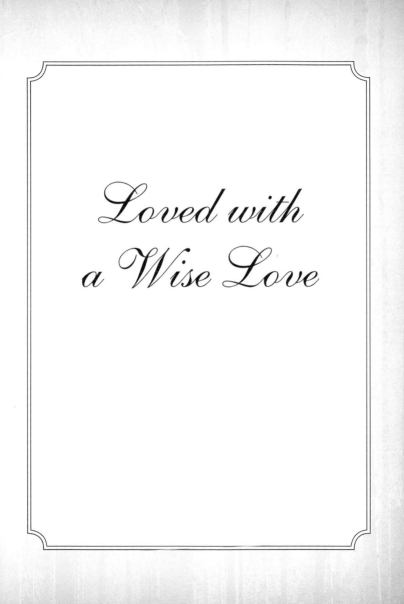

Loved with
a Wise Love

Oh, the depths of the riches of the wisdom and knowledge of God!
How unsearchable his judgments, and his paths beyond tracing out!

ROMANS 11:33 NIV

LOVED WITH A WISE LOVE

God's omniscience governs his omnipotence. Infinite knowledge rules infinite strength. "He is wise in heart, and mighty in strength" (Job 9:4 KJV). "With him is wisdom and strength" (12:13 KJV). "He is mighty in strength and wisdom" (36:5 KJV).

His power is not capricious or careless. Quite the contrary. His wisdom manages and equals his strength. Paul announced, "Oh, the depths of the riches of the wisdom and knowledge of God! How unsearchable his judgments, and his paths beyond tracing out!" (Romans 11:33 NIV).

His knowledge about you is as complete as his knowledge about the universe. "Even before a word is on my tongue, behold, O LORD, you know it altogether. . . . Your eyes saw my unformed substance; in your book were written, every one of them, the days that were formed for me, when as yet there were none of them" (Psalm 139:4, 16 ESV).

The veils that block your vision and mine do not block God's. Unspoken words are as if uttered. Unrevealed thoughts are as if proclaimed. Unoccurred moments are as if they were history. He knows the future, the past, the hidden, and the untold. Nothing is concealed from God. He is all-powerful, all-knowing, and all-present.

–*IT'S NOT ABOUT ME*

Heavenly Father, your mighty wisdom is mind-boggling. Your knowledge is complete. Nothing stumps you or perplexes you. Your wisdom is ruled by your infinite strength. You know everything about the past and the future. Nothing is hidden from you. Your mighty strength and wisdom are a firm foundation for all who believe in you. We can rely on you, as our faithful Father, to guide us, to teach us, to help us, amen.

You have hedged me behind and before, and laid Your hand upon me. Such knowledge is too wonderful for me; it is high, I cannot attain it.

PSALM 139:5–6

The LORD will perfect that which concerns me.

PSALM 138:8

"If any of you want to be my followers, you must forget about yourself. You must take up your cross each day and follow me."

LUKE 9:23 CEV

YOUR GOD-DESIGNED TASK

The phrase "take up your cross" has not fared well through the generations. Ask for a definition, and you'll hear answers like "My cross is my mother-in-law, my job, my bad marriage, my cranky boss, or the dull preacher." The cross, we assume, is any besetting affliction or personal hassle. My thesaurus agrees. It lists the following synonyms for *cross*: *frustration*, *trying situation*, *snag*, *hitch*, and *drawback*. To take up the cross is to put up with a personal challenge. God, we think, passes out crosses the way a warden hands out shovels to the chain gang. No one wants one. Each one gets one. Everybody has a cross to bear, and we might as well get used to it.

But really. Is Jesus reducing the cross to hassles and headaches? Calling us to quit complaining about the fly in the ointment or the pain in the neck? The cross means so much more. It is God's tool of redemption, instrument of salvation—proof of his love for people. To take up the cross, then, is to take up Christ's burden for the people of the world. Though our crosses are similar, none are identical. "If any of you want to be my followers, you must forget about yourself. You must take up *your cross* each day and follow me" (Luke 9:23 CEV).

We each have our own cross to carry—our individual callings. . . . It's a . . . sweet day when you discover your God-designed task. It fits. It matches your passions and enlists your gifts and talents. Want to blow the cloud cover off your gray day? Accept God's direction.

—*EVERY DAY DESERVES A CHANCE*

Lord, you have called us to take up our crosses and follow you. You challenge us to take up your burden for the people of the world. Open our eyes to see the need and open our hearts to accept our God-designed task. May our hands be willing to serve you. May we gladly give our gifts and talents to help the hurting, to feed the hungry, and to share your love with those who are lost. May we willingly forget about ourselves and find our calling in you, amen.

Therefore, my beloved brethren, be steadfast,
immovable, always abounding in the work of the Lord,
knowing that your labor is not in vain in the Lord.

1 CORINTHIANS 15:58

None of these things move me; nor do I count my life
dear to myself, so that I may finish my race with joy.

ACTS 20:24

By humility and the fear of the LORD are riches and honor and life.

PROVERBS 22:4

PURSUE HUMILITY

The story of David and Bathsheba is less a story of lust and more a story of power. A story of a man who rose too high for his own good. A man who needed to hear these words: "Come down before you fall."

"First pride, then the crash—the bigger the ego, the harder the fall" (Proverbs 16:18 MSG).

This must be why God hates arrogance. He hates to see his children fall. He hates to see his Davids seduce and his Bathshebas be victimized. God hates what pride does to his children. He doesn't dislike arrogance. He hates it. Could he state it any clearer than Proverbs 8:13: "I hate pride and arrogance" (NIV)? And then a few chapters later: "God can't stomach arrogance or pretense; believe me, he'll put those upstarts in their place" (16:5 MSG).

You don't want God to do that. . . . 'Tis far wiser to descend the mountain than fall from it.

Pursue humility. Humility doesn't mean you think less of yourself but that you think of yourself less. "Don't cherish exaggerated ideas of yourself or your importance, but try to have a sane estimate of your capabilities by the light of the faith that God has given to you" (Romans 12:3 PHILLIPS). . . .

Resist the place of celebrity. "Go sit in a seat that is not important. When the host comes to you, he may say, 'Friend, move up here to a more important place.' Then all the other guests will respect you" (Luke 14:10 NCV).

Wouldn't you rather be invited up than put down?

—*Facing Your Giants*

Heavenly Father, you have taught us in your Word that you hate pride but you honor humility. We live in a culture that feeds the natural desire to put ourselves first and to inflate our egos. It is far easier for us to be selfish than to be selfless. We need your help to live humbly in a way that pleases you. Remind us of the self-giving example of your Son, Jesus Christ. Like him, may we learn to think less of ourselves and more of others, amen.

Better to be of a humble spirit with the lowly,
than to divide the spoil with the proud.

PROVERBS 16:19

By humility and the fear of the LORD are riches and honor and life.

PROVERBS 22:4

"I am the Alpha and the Omega, the Beginning and the End," says the Lord, "who is and who was and who is to come, the Almighty."
REVELATION 1:8

GOD'S INVITATION

The hero of heaven is God. Angels don't worship mansions or glittering avenues. Neither gates nor jewels prompt the hosts to sing . . . God does. His majesty stirs the pen of heaven's poets and the awe of her citizens.

They enjoy an eternity-long answer to David's prayer: "One thing I ask of the LORD . . . to gaze upon the beauty of the LORD" (Psalm 27:4 NIV). What else warrants a look? Inhabitants of heaven forever marvel at the sins God forgives, the promises he keeps, the plan he executes. He's not the grand marshal of the parade; he is the parade. He's not the main event; he's the only event. His Broadway features a single stage and star: himself. He hosts the only production and invites every living soul to attend.

He, at this very moment, issues invitations by the millions. He whispers through the kindness of a grandparent, shouts through the tempest of a tsunami. Through the funeral he cautions, "Life is fragile." Through a sickness he reminds, "Days are numbered." God may speak through nature or nurture, majesty or mishap. But through all and to all he invites: "Come, enjoy me forever."

Yet many people have no desire to do so. They don't want anything to do with God. He speaks; they cover their ears. He commands; they scoff. They don't want him telling them how to live. They mock what he says about marriage, money, sex, or the value of human life. They regard his son as a joke and the cross as utter folly (see 1 Corinthians 1:18). They spend their lives telling God to leave them alone. And at the moment of their final breath, he honors their request: "Get away from me, you who do evil. I never knew you" (Matthew 7:23 NCV).

−3:16: THE NUMBERS OF HOPE

Holy God, we honor you as the hero of heaven. We long to be with you and gaze on your beauty. Thank you for inviting every living soul to spend eternity with you. We pray that many will come to know you and will accept you as their Lord and master. May your kingdom increase and your will be done here on earth as it is in heaven, amen.

<hr />

Blessed be the God and Father of our Lord Jesus Christ, who according to His abundant mercy has begotten us again to a living hope through the resurrection of Jesus Christ from the dead.

1 PETER 1:3

"Your heavenly Father already knows all your needs.
Seek the Kingdom of God above all else, and live righteously,
and he will give you everything you need."
MATTHEW 6:32–33 NLT

A GIFT OF TWENTY-FOUR HOURS

An hour is too short, a year too long. Days are the bite-size portions of life, the God-designed segments of life management.

Eighty-four thousand heartbeats.

One thousand four hundred and forty minutes.

A complete rotation of the earth. . . .

Both a sunrise *and* a sunset.

A brand-spanking-new, unsoiled, untouched, uncharted, and unused day!

A gift of twenty-four unlived, unexplored hours.

And if you can stack one good day on another and another, you will link together a good life.

But here's what you need to keep in mind.

You no longer have yesterday. It slipped away as you slept. It is gone. You'll more easily retrieve a puff of smoke. You can't change, alter, or improve it. Sorry, no mulligans allowed. Hourglass sand won't flow upward. The second hand of the clock refuses to tick backward. The monthly calendar reads left to right, not right to left. You no longer have yesterday.

You do not yet have tomorrow. Unless you accelerate the orbit of the earth or convince the sun to rise twice before it sets once, you can't live tomorrow today. You can't spend tomorrow's money, celebrate tomorrow's achievements, or resolve tomorrow's riddles. You have only today. *This* is the day the Lord has made.

Live in it. You must be present to win. Don't heavy today with yesterday's regrets or acidize it with tomorrow's troubles.

—Every Day Deserves a Chance

Father, you give life to us in daily portions. In your wisdom you know that twenty-four hours are sufficient for us to manage. Yet it is so easy for us to fret and fuss about what happened yesterday or to worry and fear what might happen tomorrow. You don't want us to live with guilt for failures of the past or with dread for the future. Teach us to live in the present. Remind us that you give us the wisdom and strength to live one day at a time, amen.

Come now, you who say, "Today or tomorrow we will go to such and such a city, spend a year there, buy and sell, and make a profit"; whereas you do not know what will happen tomorrow. For what is your life? It is even a vapor that appears for a little time and then vanishes away.

James 4:13–14

"Don't be afraid," he said. "Take courage. I am here!"
MATTHEW 14:27 NLT

GOD'S CALL TO COURAGE

God's call to courage is not a call to naïveté or ignorance. We aren't to be oblivious to the overwhelming challenges that life brings. We're to counterbalance them with long looks at God's accomplishments. "We must pay much closer attention to what we have heard, so that we do not drift away from it" (Hebrews 2:1 NASB). Do whatever it takes to keep your gaze on Jesus.

When a friend of mine spent several days in the hospital at the bedside of her husband, she relied on hymns to keep her spirits up. Every few minutes, she stepped into the restroom and sang a few verses of "Great Is Thy Faithfulness." Do likewise! Memorize scripture. Read biographies of great lives. Ponder the testimonies of faithful Christians. Make the deliberate decision to set your hope on him. Courage is always a possibility. . . .

As followers of God, you and I have a huge asset. We know everything is going to turn out all right. Christ hasn't budged from his throne, and Romans 8:28 hasn't evaporated from the Bible. Our problems have always been his possibilities. The kidnapping of Joseph resulted in the preservation of his family. The persecution of Daniel led to a cabinet position. Christ entered the world by a surprise pregnancy and redeemed it through his unjust murder. Dare we believe what the Bible teaches? That no disaster is ultimately fatal?

Feed your fears, and your faith will starve.

Feed your faith, and your fears will.

—Fearless

Holy Father, you call us to courage. Your Word assures that nothing comes our way that you have not allowed. The Bible teaches that our problems are your possibilities. Help us remember to feed our faith by reading your Word. We set our hope on you, amen.

Nothing can ever separate us from God's love. Neither death nor life, neither angels nor demons, neither our fears for today nor our worries about tomorrow—not even the powers of hell can separate us from God's love.

ROMANS 8:38 NLT

"I am with you always, to the very end of the age."

MATTHEW 28:20 NIV

Why should you . . . be enraptured by an immoral woman,
and be embraced in the arms of a seductress?

PROVERBS 5:20

THE PROTECTIVE FENCE OF FIDELITY

Casual sex, intimacy outside of marriage, pulls the Corinthian ploy. It pretends we can give the body and not affect the soul. We can't. We humans are so intricately psychosomatic that whatever touches the *soma* impacts the *psyche* as well. The me-centered phrase "as long as no one gets hurt" sounds noble, but the truth is, we don't know who gets hurt. God-centered thinking rescues us from the sex we thought would make us happy. You may think your dalliances are harmless, and years may pass before the x-rays reveal the internal damage, but don't be fooled. Casual sex is a diet of chocolate—it tastes good for a while, but the imbalance can ruin you. Sex apart from God's plan wounds the soul.

Sex according to God's plan nourishes the soul. Consider his plan. Two children of God make a covenant with each other. They disable the ejection seats. They burn the bridge back to Momma's house. They fall into each other's arms beneath the canopy of God's blessing, encircled by the tall fence of fidelity. Both know the other will be there in the morning. Both know the other will stay even as skin wrinkles and vigor fades. Each gives the other exclusive for-your-eyes only privileges. Gone is the guilt. Gone the undisciplined lust. What remains is a celebration of permanence, a tender moment in which the body continues what the mind and the soul have already begun. A time in which "the man and his wife were both naked and were not ashamed" (Genesis 2:25 NASB).

Such sex honors God. And such sex satisfies God's children.

–*It's Not About Me*

Heavenly Father, you created marriage and gave us guidelines for that relationship. Because of your great love, you gave us these guidelines for our own well-being. You want to protect us from heartbreak and remorse. Help us to heed your words, Father, and to be obedient to your commands about sex. May every act of our lives, whether physical or spiritual, bring honor and glory to you, amen.

Rejoice with the wife of your youth. As a loving deer
and a graceful doe, let her breasts satisfy you at all times;
and always be enraptured with her love.

PROVERBS 5:18–19

God is able to provide you with every blessing in abundance.
2 CORINTHIANS 9:8 RSV

GOD ALREADY HAS A PLAN

If your father were Bill Gates and your computer broke, where would you turn? If Stradivari were your dad and your violin string snapped, to whom would you go? If your father is God and you have a problem on your hands, what do you do?

Scripture tells us what to do:

- Is your problem too large? "God . . . is able . . . to accomplish infinitely more than we might ask or think" (Ephesians 3:20 NLT).
- Is your need too great? "God is able to provide you with every blessing in abundance" (2 Corinthians 9:8 RSV).
- Is your temptation too severe? "[God] is able to help us when we are being tested" (Hebrews 2:18 NLT).
- Are your sins too numerous? "He is able, once and forever, to save those who come to God through him" (Hebrews 7:25 NLT).
- Is your future too frightening? "God . . . is able to keep you from falling away and will bring you with great joy into his glorious presence without a single fault" (Jude 24 NLT).

- Is your enemy too strong? "[God] is able even to subdue all things to Himself" (Philippians 3:21).

Make these verses a part of your daily dict. God is able to accomplish, provide, help, save, keep, subdue. . . . He is able to do what you can't. He already has a plan. God's not bewildered. Go to him.

—EVERY DAY DESERVES A CHANCE

Father God, you are a strong and kind father to your children. You are concerned about the smallest detail of our lives. You have numbered the hairs of our heads. You are all-knowing and all-powerful. There is nothing too hard for you. May we never forget that you are always present with us and always ready to hear the cries of our hearts. No problem we face is unimportant to you. No facet of our lives is too big or too small to bring to you. We praise you for being our faithful, loving heavenly Father, amen.

"For I know the plans I have for you," declares the Lord, "plans to prosper you and not to harm you, plans to give you hope and a future."

JEREMIAH 29:11

He is also able to save to the uttermost those who come to God through Him, since He always lives to make intercession for them.

HEBREWS 7:25

Let the words of Christ, in all their richness,
live in your hearts and make you wise.

"YOUR SERVANT IS LISTENING"

Has any other book ever been described in this fashion: "For the word of God is living and active. Sharper than any double-edged sword, it penetrates even to dividing soul and spirit, joints and marrow; it judges the thoughts and attitudes of the heart" (Hebrews 4:12 NIV)?

"Living and active." The words of the Bible have life! Nouns with pulse rates. Muscular adjectives. Verbs darting back and forth across the page. God works though these words. The Bible is to God what a surgical glove is to the surgeon. He reaches through them to touch deep within you.

Haven't you felt his touch?

In a late, lonely hour, you read the words "I will never fail you. I will never abandon you" (Hebrews 13:5 NLT). The sentences comfort like a hand on your shoulder.

When anxiety termites away at your peace, someone shares this passage: "Do not be anxious about anything, but in everything, by prayer and petition, with thanksgiving, present your requests to God" (Philippians 4:6 NIV). The words stir a sigh from your soul.

Put them to use. "Let the words of Christ, in all their richness, live in your hearts and make you wise. Use his words to teach and counsel each other" (Colossians 3:16 NLT).

Don't make a decision, whether large or small, without sitting before God with open Bible, open heart, open ears, imitating the prayer of Samuel: "Your servant is listening" (1 Samuel 3:10 NLT).

—*Facing Your Giants*

Precious Lord, your Word is an awesome treasure. It is filled with words to guide, to instruct, and to comfort us. Your holy Word is powerful and as true today as when it was written. Thank you for this truly amazing gift. May we never let one day pass without reading the Bible. Please open our hearts and minds to hear what you want to say through your Word. We are listening, Lord, amen.

He who heeds the word wisely will find good,
and whoever trusts in the LORD, happy is he.

PROVERBS 16:20

Great peace have those who love Your law,
and nothing causes them to stumble.

PSALM 119:165

Yes, and everyone who wants to live a godly life
in Christ Jesus will suffer persecution.

2 TIMOTHY 3:12 NLT

STRENGTH AND COURAGE

"Now when [the accusers] saw the boldness of Peter and John, and perceived that they were uneducated and untrained men, they marveled. And they realized that they had been with Jesus" (Acts 4:13).

Peter and John had been with Jesus. The resurrected Jesus. In the Upper Room when he walked through the wall. Standing next to Thomas when the disciple touched the wounds. On the beach when Jesus cooked the fish. Sitting at Jesus' feet for forty days as he explained the ways of the kingdom.

They had lingered long and delightfully in the presence of the resurrected King. Awakening with him, walking with him. And because they had, silence was no longer an option. "We cannot but speak the things which we have seen and heard" (v. 20).

Could you use some high-octane boldness? If you want to outlive your life, you could. As long as you are stationary, no one will complain. Dogs don't bark at parked cars. But as soon as you accelerate—once you step out of drunkenness into sobriety, dishonesty into integrity, or lethargy into compassion—expect the yapping to begin. Expect to be criticized. Expect to be mocked. Expect to be persecuted.

So how can we prepare ourselves? Simple. Imitate the disciples. Linger long and often in the presence of Christ. Meditate on his grace. Ponder his love. Memorize his words. Gaze into his face. Talk to him. Courage comes as we live with Jesus.

Peter said it this way. "Don't give the opposition a second thought. Through thick and thin, keep your hearts at attention, in adoration before Christ, your Master. Be ready to speak up and tell anyone who asks why you're living the way you are, and always with the utmost courtesy" (1 Peter 3:14–15 MSG).

As we meditate on Christ's life, we find strength for our own.

–OUTLIVE YOUR LIFE

Father, help us to be bold for you like Peter and John. May our lives count for your kingdom. Outfit us with courage to overcome tests and trials. We will meditate on your grace and ponder your love. You, Lord, are the center of our lives, amen.

Be strong and of good courage; do not be afraid, nor be dismayed, for the LORD your God is with you wherever you go.

JOSHUA 1:9

The heavens declare the glory of God;
and the firmament shows His handiwork.

PSALM 19:1

LOVED BY GOD THE CREATOR

Venture away from the city lights on a clear night, and look up at the sky. That fuzzy band of white light is our galaxy, the Milky Way. One hundred billion stars.[14] Our galaxy is one of billions of others![15] Who can conceive of such a universe, let alone infinite numbers of universes?

No one can. But let's try anyway. Suppose you attempt to drive to the sun. A car dealer offers you a sweet deal on a space vehicle (no doubt solar powered) that averages 150 miles per hour. You hop in, open the moonroof, and blast off. You drive nonstop, twenty-four hours a day, 365 days a year. Any guess as to the length of your trip? Try seventy years! Suppose, after stretching your legs and catching a bit of sun, you fuel up and rocket off to Alpha Centauri, the next closest star system. Best pack a lunch and clear your calendar. You'll need 15 million years to make the trip.[16]

Don't like to drive, you say? Board a jet, and zip through our solar system at a blistering six hundred miles per hour. In 16.5 days you'll reach the moon, in seventeen years you'll pass the sun, and in 690 years you can enjoy dinner on Pluto. After seven centuries you haven't even left our solar system, much less our galaxy.[17]

Our universe is God's preeminent missionary. "The heavens declare the glory of God" (Psalm 19:1 NIV). A house implies a builder; a painting suggests a painter. Don't stars suggest a star maker? Doesn't creation imply a creator? "The heavens declare His righteousness" (Psalm 97:6). Look above you. . . .

If God can make a billion galaxies, can't he make good out of our bad and sense out of our faltering lives? Of course he can. He is God.

—3:16: THE NUMBERS OF HOPE

Heavenly Father, your creative powers are mind-boggling. The universe you have created is beyond comprehension. You created everything by your mighty power, and you sustain everything by that same power. How comforting to know that you can create galaxies and yet you care about every detail in my life. What a privilege to trust in your loving power no matter what comes my way, amen.

<hr>

You, LORD, in the beginning laid the foundation of the earth, and the heavens are the work of Your hands. They will perish, but You remain.

HEBREWS 1:10–11

"He who endures to the end shall be saved."

MATTHEW 24:13

FARSIGHTED COURAGE

Life is a dangerous endeavor. We pass our days in the shadows of ominous realities. The power to annihilate humanity has, it seems, been placed in the hands of people who are happy to do so. . . . If the global temperature rises a few more degrees . . . if classified information falls into sinister hands . . . if the wrong person pushes the wrong red button . . . What if things only get worse?

Christ tells us that they will. He predicts spiritual bailouts, ecological turmoil, and worldwide persecution. Yet in the midst of it all, he contends bravery is still an option. "Watch out that no one deceives you. For many will come in my name, claiming, 'I am the Christ,' and will deceive many. You will hear of wars and rumors of wars, but see to it that you are not alarmed" (Matthew 24:46 NIV).

Things are going to get bad, really bad, before they get better. And when conditions worsen, "See to it that you are not alarmed" (v. 6 NIV). Jesus chose a stout term for *alarmed* that he used on no other occasion. It means "to wail, to cry aloud," as if Jesus counseled the disciples, "Don't freak out when bad stuff happens." . . .

Don't freak out at the heresy, calamity, and apostasy. Don't give in or give up, for you'll soon witness the victory. "But he who endures to the end shall be saved. And this gospel of the kingdom will be preached in all the world as a witness to all the nations, and then the end will come" (vv. 13–14).

Jesus equipped his followers with farsighted courage. He listed the typhoons of life and then pointed them "to the end." Trust in ultimate victory gives ultimate courage.

—*Fearless*

Some days, holy Father, it seems that the world is spinning out of control. Worldwide turmoil increases, and we are alarmed. It is easy to lose courage. But this is not what you want for your children. You have given us ample warning that these things will happen. May we remember that they are preparations for the end of time. When we forget, remind us that ultimate victory belongs to you. Help us face the future with courage and confidence, amen.

The LORD shall preserve you from all evil; He shall preserve your soul.

PSALM 121:7

Always be joyful. Pray continually, and give thanks whatever happens. That is what God wants for you in Christ Jesus.

1 THESSALONIANS 5:16—18 NCV

A GRATEFUL HEART

God notices the grateful heart. Why? Does he have an ego problem? No. But we do. Gratitude lifts our eyes off the things we lack so we might see the blessings we possess. Nothing blows the winter out of the day like the Caribbean breeze of thankfulness. Need some trade winds?

Major in the grace of God. When Paul sent Timothy off to spiritual university, he told him to major in the grace of God: "You therefore, my son, *be strong in the grace* that is in Christ Jesus" (2 Timothy 2:1). Do the same. Focus on the cross of Christ. Grow fluent in the language of redemption. Linger long at the foot of the cross. Immerse yourself in the curriculum of grace. And . . .

Measure the gifts of God. Collect your blessings. Catalog his kindnesses. Assemble your reasons for gratitude and recite them. "Always be joyful. Pray continually, and give thanks whatever happens. That is what God wants for you in Christ Jesus" (1 Thessalonians 5:16–18 NCV). Look at the totality of those terms. *Always be joyful. Pray continually. Give thanks whatever happens.*

—*EVERY DAY DESERVES A CHANCE*

Heavenly Father, too often we concentrate on the weeds in life even when we live in the garden of your grace. Help us remember that gratitude is always an option. Whatever comes our way, may we choose to give thanks to you. When we forget, remind us of the innumerable blessings you have poured into our lives. When we remember your gifts to us, we can't help but be filled with gratitude and joy. Teach us to rejoice in all things, amen.

Let us continually offer the sacrifice of praise to God,
that is, the fruit of our lips, giving thanks to His name.

HEBREWS 13:15

In everything give thanks; for this is the will
of God in Christ Jesus for you.

1 THESSALONIANS 5:18

Continue earnestly in prayer, being vigilant in it with thanksgiving.

COLOSSIANS 4:2

Pour out your heart like water before the face of the Lord. Lift your hands toward Him for the life of your young children.

LAMENTATIONS 2:19

PRAYING PARENTS

Parents, we can do this. We can be loyal advocates, stubborn intercessors. We can take our parenting fears to Christ. In fact, if we don't, we'll take our fears out on our kids. Fear turns some parents into paranoid prison guards who monitor every minute, check the background of every friend. They stifle growth and communicate distrust. A family with no breathing room suffocates a child.

On the other hand, fear can also create permissive parents. For fear that their child will feel too confined or fenced in, they lower all boundaries. High on hugs and low on discipline. They don't realize that appropriate discipline is an expression of love. Permissive parents. Paranoid parents. How can we avoid the extremes? We pray.

Prayer is the saucer into which parental fears are poured to cool. Jesus says so little about parenting, makes no comments about spanking, breast-feeding, sibling rivalry, or schooling. Yet his actions speak volumes about prayer. Each time a parent prays, Christ responds. His big message to moms and dads? Bring your children to me. Raise them in a greenhouse of prayer.

—*FEARLESS*

Lord Jesus, when you were here on earth, you showed tender love for children. You protected them and defended them. May we be as dedicated and devoted to our own children. When we begin to worry and be anxious for them, teach us to talk to you about our fears. Lord, you love our children even more than we do. You want what is best for them even more than we do. We can trust you to take care of our children and to guide us as we seek to be godly parents, amen.

All your children shall be taught by the LORD,
and great shall be the peace of your children.

ISAIAH 54:13

The eyes of the LORD are on the righteous,
and His ears are open to their prayers.

1 PETER 3:12

"Whatever you do, do all to the glory of God."

1 CORINTHIANS 10:31

PROCLAIM GOD'S GLORY

Whatever? Whatever.

Let your message reflect his glory. "Let your light shine before men, that they may see your good deeds and praise your Father in heaven" (Matthew 5:16 NIV).

Let your salvation reflect God's glory. "Having believed, you were marked in him with a seal, the promised Holy Spirit, who is a deposit guaranteeing our inheritance until the redemption of those who are God's possession—to the praise of his glory" (Ephesians 1:13–14 NIV).

Let your body reflect God's glory. "You are not your own. . . . Glorify God in your body" (1 Corinthians 6:19–20 NASB).

Your struggles. "These sufferings of ours are for your benefit. And the more of you who are won to Christ, the more there are to thank him for his great kindness, and the more the Lord is glorified" (2 Corinthians 4:15 TLB; see also John 11:4).

Your success honors God. "Honor the LORD with your wealth" (Proverbs 3:9 NIV). "Riches and honor come from you" (1 Chronicles 29:12 NCV). "God . . . is giving you power to make wealth" (Deuteronomy 8:18 NASB).

Your message, your salvation, your body, your struggles, your success—all proclaim God's glory.

–It's Not About Me

Gracious Father, we pray that every facet of our lives would bring glory to you. We want to honor you with every struggle we face as well as every success. May our words and actions uplift your name. May the testimony of our own salvation draw others to you. May our lives be consistent proclamations of your glory. You deserve all the honor and praise, amen.

Whatever you do in word or deed, do all in the name of the Lord Jesus,
giving thanks through Him to God the Father.

Colossians 3:17 nasb

If you live according to the flesh you will die; but if by
the Spirit you put to death the deeds of the body, you will live.

Romans 8:13

Walk in the Spirit, and you shall not fulfill the lust of the flesh.

Galatians 5:16

He who follows righteousness and mercy finds life,
righteousness and honor.

PROVERBS 21:21

THE DEPTHS OF GOD'S LOVE

People can exhaust you. And there are times when all we can do is not enough. When a spouse chooses to leave, we cannot force him or her to stay. When a spouse abuses, we shouldn't stay. The best of love can go unrequited. I don't for a moment intend to minimize the challenges some of you face. You're tired. You're angry. You're disappointed. This isn't the marriage you expected or the life you wanted. But looming in your past is a promise you made. May I urge you to do all you can to keep it? To give it one more try?

Why should you? So you can understand the depth of God's love.

When you love the unloving, you get a glimpse of what God does for you. When you keep the porch light on for the prodigal child, when you do what is right even though you have been done wrong, when you love the weak and the sick, you do what God does every single moment. Covenant-keeping enrolls you in the postgraduate school of God's love.

Is this why God has given you this challenge? When you love liars, cheaters, and heartbreakers, are you not doing what God has done for us? Pay attention to and take notes on your struggles. God invites you to understand his love.

–FACING YOUR GIANTS

Father God, we can't fathom the depth and height and strength of your love. It cannot be measured. Your love reaches beyond the highest heavens and is deeper than the deepest sea. Your love is consistent and steadfast. Father, you don't love us more one day and less the next. Open our eyes to see every struggle in life as an opportunity to show your love and to better understand your love. Teach us to love with a servant's heart, amen.

"A new commandment I give to you, that you love one another; as I have loved you, that you also love one another."

JOHN 13:34

As each one has received a gift, minister it to one another, as good stewards of the manifold grace of God.

1 PETER 4:10

*Search me, O God, and know my heart; test me and know
my anxious thoughts. Point out anything in me that offends you,
and lead me along the path of everlasting life.*

Psalm 139:23—24 NLT

SLAY THE DESIRE TO BE NOTICED

When people enter a church to see God yet can't see God because of the church, don't think for a second that God doesn't react. "Be especially careful when you are trying to be good so that you don't make a performance out of it. It might be good theater, but the God who made you won't be applauding" (Matthew 6:1 MSG).

Hypocrisy turns people against God. So God has a no-tolerance policy. Let's take hypocrisy as seriously as God does. How can we?

1. Expect no credit for good deeds. None. If no one notices, you aren't disappointed. If someone does, you give the credit to God.

2. Give financial gifts in secret. Money stirs the phony within us. We like to be seen earning it. And we like to be seen giving it. So "when you give to someone in need, don't let your left hand know what your right hand is doing" (v. 3 NLT).

3. Don't fake spirituality. When you go to church, don't select a seat just to be seen or sing just to be heard. If you raise your hands in worship, raise holy ones, not showy ones. When you talk, don't doctor your vocabulary with trendy religious terms. Nothing nauseates more than a fake "Praise the Lord" or a shallow "Hallelujah" or an insincere "Glory be to God."

Bottom line: don't make a theater production out of your faith. "Watch me! Watch me!" is a call used on the playground, not in God's kingdom. Silence the trumpets. Cancel the parade. Enough with the name-dropping. If accolades come, politely deflect them before you believe them. Slay the desire to be noticed. Stir the desire to serve God.

Do good things. Just don't do them to be noticed. You can be too good for your own good, you know.

–*Outlive Your Life*

Lord Jesus, forgive us for the times we have faked spirituality and participated out of pride. Forgive us for acts done to be seen or to receive praise. Give us hearts that are humble and willing to serve you in secret. May we be quick to give you all the honor and glory. May your church reflect you, for the sake of the lost and for our own sakes, amen.

For our boasting is this: the testimony of our conscience that we conducted ourselves in the world in simplicity and godly sincerity, not with fleshy wisdom but by the grace of God. . . .

2 Corinthians 1:12

"If anyone desires to be first, he shall be last of all and servant of all."

THE INGREDIENT OF A GREAT DAY

We regularly face subtle yet significant decisions, all of which fall under the category of who comes first: do they or do I?

When the parent chooses the best school for the children over a career-advancing transfer.

When the student eats lunch with the neglected kids rather than the cool ones.

When the grown daughter spends her days off with her aging mother at the dementia unit.

When you turn away from personal dreams for the sake of others, you are, in Christ's words, denying yourself. "If any of you wants to be my follower, you must turn from your selfish ways, take up your cross, and follow me" (Matthew 16:24 NLT).

Behold the most surprising ingredient of a great day: self-denial.

Don't we assume just the opposite? Great days emerge from the soil of self-indulgence, self-expression, and self-celebration. So pamper yourself, indulge yourself, promote yourself. But deny yourself? When was the last time you read this ad copy: "Go ahead. Deny yourself and have the time of your life!"?

Jesus could have written the words. He often goes countercultural, calling us down rather than up, telling us to zig when society says to zag.

In his economy the least are the greatest (Luke 9:48); the last will be first (Mark 9:35); the chosen seats are the forgotten seats (Luke 14:8–9). He tells us to honor others above ourselves (Romans 12:10); and consider others better than ourselves (Philippians 2:3).

—*Every Day Deserves a Chance*

O Lord, your Word teaches us to deny ourselves. But our natural tendency is to indulge ourselves, to seek our own interests rather than the interests of others. We know this does not please you, for you have taught us that the least are the greatest and the last will be first. When we have opportunities to make a decision about who comes first, fill our hearts with a sacrificial love that will choose to put others first, amen.

Let nothing be done through selfish ambition or conceit, but in lowliness of mind let each esteem others better than himself.

PHILIPPIANS 2:3

O my Strength, I will sing praises to you, for you, O God,
are my fortress, the God who shows me steadfast love.

PSALM 59:17 ESV

A STRONG HAND TO HOLD

With life comes change.

With change comes fear, insecurity, sorrow, stress. So what do you do? Hibernate? Take no risks for fear of failing? Give no love for fear of losing? Some opt to. They hold back.

A better idea is to look up. Set your bearings on the one and only North Star in the universe—God. For though life changes, he never does. Scripture makes pupil-popping claims about his permanence.

Consider his strength. Unending. According to Paul, God's power lasts forever (Romans 1:20). His strength never diminishes. Yours and mine will and has. Our energy ebbs and flows more than the Thames River. You aren't as alert in the evening as in the morning. You can't run as fast when you are eighty as when you are twenty. . . . You are strong, but you won't be strong forever.

God will. The words "I'm feeling strong today" he has never said. He feels equally strong every day.

Daniel calls him "the living God, enduring forever" (Daniel 6:26 ESV). The psalmist tells him, "I will sing of your strength. . . . For you have been to me a fortress and a refuge in the day of my distress. O my Strength, I will sing praises to you, for you, O God, are my fortress, the God who shows me steadfast love" (Psalm 59:16–17 ESV).

Think about it. God never pauses to eat or asks the angels to cover for him while he naps. He never signals a time-out or puts the prayer requests from Russia on hold while he handles South Africa. He "never slumbers or never sleeps" (Psalm 121:4 NLT). Need a strong hand to hold? You'll always find one in his. His strength never changes.

–IT'S NOT ABOUT ME

Heavenly Father, you are the North Star of the universe. Your strength is unending and your power lasts forever. You are a fortress and refuge to all who call on you for help. You are always available and always the same. When we face changes in life that bring insecurity and stress, teach us to take our worries and fear to you, to depend on you, amen.

He will not allow your foot to be moved;
He who keeps you will not slumber.

PSALM 121:3

God is my salvation and my glory; the rock of my strength.

PSALM 62:7

The LORD does not see as man sees; for man looks at the outward appearance, but the LORD looks at the heart.

A GOD-SEEKING HEART

"The LORD does not see as man sees; for man looks at the outward appearance, but the LORD looks at the heart" (1 Samuel 16:7).

Those words were written for the . . . misfits and outcasts of society. God uses them all.

Moses ran from justice, but God used him.

Jonah ran from God, but God used him.

Rahab ran a brothel, Samson ran to the wrong woman, Jacob ran in circles, Elijah ran into the mountains, Sarah ran out of hope, Lot ran with the wrong crowd, but God used them all.

And David? God saw a teenage boy serving him in the backwoods of Bethlehem, at the intersection of boredom and anonymity, and through the voice of a brother, God called, "David! Come in. Someone wants to see you." Human eyes saw a gangly teenager enter the house, smelling like sheep and looking like he needed a bath. Yet, "the LORD said, 'Arise, anoint him; for this is the one!'" (1 Samuel 16:12).

God saw what no one else saw: a God-seeking heart. David, for all his foibles, sought God like a lark seeks sunrise. He took after God's heart because he stayed after God's heart. In the end, that's all God wanted or needed . . . wants or needs. Others measure your waist size or wallet. Not God. He examines hearts. When he finds one set on him, he calls it and claims it.

—FACING YOUR GIANTS

Gracious God, thank you for loving the misfits of society and for using them in your kingdom. You used outcasts of society like Moses and Jonah and Rahab and David. You still use those whose hearts are set firmly on you whether they are approved by society or not. While people judge us by looks or talents or accomplishments or wealth, you look at our hearts. We long to seek more strongly after you, O God. Help us to be people who seek you above all else, amen.

"I am the vine, you are the branches. He who abides in Me, and I in him, bears much fruit; for without Me you can do nothing."

JOHN 15:5

But seek first the Kingdom of God and His righteousness, and all these shall be added to you.

MATTHEW 6:33

By those who come near Me I must be regarded as holy;
and before all the people I must be glorified.

LEVITICUS 10:3

GOD'S PRIORITY

The Hebrew term for *glory* descends from a root word meaning heavy, weighty, or important. God's glory, then, celebrates his significance, his uniqueness, his one-of-a-kindness. As Moses prayed, "Who among the gods is like you, O LORD? Who is like you—majestic in holiness, awesome in glory, working wonders?" (Exodus 15:11 NIV).

When you think "God's glory," think "preeminence." And when you think "preeminence," think "priority." For God's glory is God's priority.

God's staff meetings, if he had them, would revolve around one question: "How can we reveal my glory today?" God's to-do list consists of one item: "Reveal my glory." Heaven's framed and mounted purpose statement hangs in the angels' break room just above the angel food cake. It reads: "Declare God's glory."

God exists to showcase God.

He told Moses: "By those who come near Me I must be regarded as holy; and before all the people I must be glorified" (Leviticus 10:3). . . .

164

Why do the heavens exist? The heavens exist to "declare the glory of God" (Psalm 19:1 NIV).

Why did God choose the Israelites? Through Isaiah he called out to "everyone who is called by My name, and whom I have created for My glory" (Isaiah 43:7 NASB).

Why do people struggle? God answers, "I have tested you in the furnace of affliction. For My own sake, for My own sake, I will act" (48:10–11 NASB). "Then call on me when you are in trouble, and I will rescue you, and you will give me glory" (Psalm 50:15 NLT).

—It's Not About Me

Blessed Father, you are glorious and mighty. You are majestic in pure holiness and awesome power. We praise your goodness and your greatness. You alone are worthy to receive all of our thanksgiving and adoration. You are worthy of our trust. We turn to you with our tears and know you hear the cry of our hearts. You hear and you care. May our lives, like the heavens, declare your glory each and every day, amen.

Ascribe to the Lord the glory due his name;
worship the Lord in the splendor of his holiness.

PSALM 29:2 NIV

*"Please take this cup of suffering away from me.
Yet I want your will to be done, not mine."*

MARK 14:36 NLT

FACE FEAR WITH HONEST PRAYER

Jesus did more than speak about fear. He faced it.

The decisive acts of the gospel drama are played out on two stages—Gethsemane's garden and Golgotha's cross. Friday's cross witnessed the severest suffering. Thursday's garden staged the profoundest fear. It was here, amidst the olive trees, that Jesus "fell to the ground. He prayed that, if it were possible, the awful hour awaiting him might pass him by. 'Abba, Father,' he cried out, 'everything is possible for you. Please take this cup of suffering away from me. Yet I want your will to be done, not mine'" (Mark 14:35–36 NLT). . . .

Of what was Jesus afraid? . . .

The cup equaled Jesus' worst-case scenario: to be the recipient of God's wrath. He had never felt God's fury, didn't deserve to. He'd never experienced isolation from his Father; the two had been one for eternity. He'd never known physical death; he was an immortal being. Yet within a few short hours, Jesus would face them all. God would unleash his sin-hating wrath on the sin-covered Son. And Jesus was afraid. Deathly afraid. And what he did with his fear shows us what to do with ours.

He prayed. He told his followers, "Sit here while I go and pray over there" (Matthew 26:36). One prayer was inadequate. "Again, a second time, He went away and prayed. . . . And prayed the third time, saying the same words" (vv. 42, 44). He even requested the prayer support of his friends. "Stay awake and pray for strength," he urged (v. 41 NCV).

Jesus faced his ultimate fear with honest prayer.

—*FEARLESS*

Lord, when you were confronted with a fearful situation, you faced it with honest prayer. Grant us the wisdom and the strength to do the same. No matter how frightening the circumstance, may we choose to share it with you in sincere and simple prayer. Before we turn anywhere else, may we turn to you. By the comfort of your Holy Spirit, may we find peace and hope and joy, amen.

For He Himself has said, "I will never leave you nor forsake you."

HEBREWS 13:5

Commit your way to the LORD, trust also in Him,
and He shall bring it to pass.

PSALM 37:5

Rejoice in the Lord always. Again I will say, rejoice!

PHILIPPIANS 4:4

REMEMBER WHO'S IN CHARGE

The praetorian guard was a handpicked division of crack imperial troops. They received double pay and added benefits. They were the finest of the fine. And, in God's sovereignty, the finest of Caesar's soldiers are chained to the finest of God's. How much time passed before Paul realized what was happening? How long before Paul looked at the chains, looked at the bright West Point graduate, and then smiled a smile toward heaven? *Hmm.* Captive audience. He leans toward the soldier. "Got a minute to talk?" Or "Would you mind proofreading this letter I'm writing?" or "Can I tell you about a Jewish carpenter I know?"

His words meet their mark. Read this line from the Philippian benediction: "All of God's people greet you, particularly those from the palace of Caesar" (4:22 NCV).

The man may be manacled, but the message is not. The prison of Paul becomes the pulpit of Paul, and that is fine with him. Any method is fine as long as Christ is preached. . . .

Paul can write from the chill of the jail, "So I am happy, and I will continue to be happy" (1:18 NCV).

Unfairly arrested. Unkindly treated. Uncharted future. Yet unbridled joy.

Bumped off track but still in the race. How? We can summarize all the reasons with one word. Reduce all the answers to a single verb. Distill the explanations into one decision.

What is the word, verb, and decision? *Trust.*

Paul trusted the oversight of God. He didn't know why bad things happened. He didn't know how they would be resolved. But he knew who was in charge.

Knowing who's in charge counterbalances the mystery of why and how.

—*Every Day Deserves a Chance*

Dear Lord Jesus, each day of life seems to bring a new challenge. Many of these are difficult trials that test us to the limit. We don't understand why these things happen or how they happen. But like the apostle Paul, we want to declare in all circumstances that we are happy in you and will continue to be happy. Help us to leave the oversight of our situations to you. Remind us that you are in charge and we can trust completely in your loving grace and compassion, amen.

Not that we are sufficient of ourselves to think anything as being from ourselves, but our sufficiency is from God.

2 Corinthians 3:5

If anyone is in Christ, he is a new creation;
old things have passed away; behold, all things have become new.

2 CORINTHIANS 5:17

JESUS OFFERS ANSWERS

One of my Boy Scout assignments was to build a kite. One of my blessings as a Boy Scout was a kite-building dad. He built a lot of things: scooters on skates, go-carts. Why, he even built our house. A kite to him was stick figures to van Gogh. Could handle them in his sleep.

With wood glue, poles, and newspaper, we fashioned a sky-dancing masterpiece: red, white, and blue and shaped like a box. We launched our creation on the back of a March wind. But after some minutes, my kite caught a downdraft and plunged. I tightened the string, raced in reverse, and did all I could to maintain elevation. But it was too late. She Hindenburged earthward.

Envision a redheaded, heartsick twelve-year-old standing over his collapsed kite. That was me. Envision a square-bodied man with ruddy skin and coveralls placing his hand on the boy's shoulder. That was my kite-making dad. He surveyed the heap of sticks and paper and assured, "It's okay. We can fix this." I believed him. Why not? He spoke with authority.

So does Christ. To all whose lives feel like a crashed kite, he says, "We can fix this. Let me teach you. Let me teach you how to handle your money, long Mondays, and cranky in-laws. Let me teach you why people fight, death comes, and forgiveness counts. But most of all, let me teach you why on earth you are on this earth."

Don't we need to learn? We know so much, and yet we know so little. The age of information is the age of confusion: much know-how, hardly any know-why. We need answers. Jesus offers them.

—3:16: The Numbers of Hope

Gracious Lord, when life falls apart around us, may we turn to you and let you fix it. Sometimes we want to take things into our own hands and fix everything ourselves. But help us remember that you are the amazing Lord of the universe who holds all the answers we need. You are a proven answer to life's problems and a source of strength for life's struggles. Without you our lives would be empty and futile, amen.

Let us hold fast the confession of our hope without wavering, for He who promised is faithful.

Hebrews 10:23

God has not given us a spirit of fear,
but of power and of love and of a sound mind.
2 TIMOTHY 1:7

REPLACE FEAR WITH FAITH

Fear never wrote a symphony or poem, negotiated a peace treaty, or cured a disease. Fear never pulled a family out of poverty or a country out of bigotry. Fear never saved a marriage or a business. Courage did that. Faith did that. People who refused to consult or cower to their timidities did that. . . .

To be clear, fear serves a healthy function. It is the canary in the coal mine, warning of potential danger. A dose of fright can keep a child from running across a busy road or an adult from smoking a pack of cigarettes. Fear is the appropriate reaction to a burning building or growling dog. Fear itself is not a sin. But it can lead to sin.

If we medicate fear with angry outbursts, drinking binges, sullen withdrawals, self-starvation, or viselike control, we exclude God from the solution and exacerbate the problem. We subject ourselves to a position of fear, allowing anxiety to dominate and define our lives. Joy-sapping worries. Day-numbing dread. Repeated bouts of insecurity that petrify and paralyze us. Hysteria is not from God. "For God has not given us a *spirit* of fear" (2 Timothy 1:7).

Fear may fill our world, but it doesn't have to fill our hearts. It will always knock on the door. Just don't invite it in for dinner, and for heaven's sake don't offer it a bed for the night.

—*FEARLESS*

Father God let our thoughts and actions reflect a confidence in you. May we not be overwhelmed by fear and anxiety. We know that hysteria does not come from you and it does not please you. Fill our hearts instead with faith. Remind us that you are our loving Father. May we never forget that you care for every detail of our lives and we can cast all our cares on you. You are our refuge, our home, amen.

For you did not receive the spirit of bondage again to fear, but you received the Spirit of adoption by whom we cry out, "Abba, Father."

ROMANS 8:15

For the eyes of the LORD run to and fro throughout the whole earth, to show Himself strong on behalf of those whose heart is loyal to Him.

2 CHRONICLES 16:9

God is kind to you so you will change your hearts and lives.

ROMANS 2:4 NCV

IN THE IMAGE OF CHRIST

Here's God's agenda for your day: to make you more like Jesus.

"God…decided from the outset to shape the lives of those who love him along the same lines as the life of his Son" (Romans 8:29 MSG). Do you see what God is doing? Shaping you "along the same lines as the life of his Son."

Jesus felt no guilt; God wants you to feel no guilt.

Jesus had no bad habits; God wants to do away with yours.

Jesus faced fears with courage; God wants you to do the same.

Jesus knew the difference between right and wrong; God wants us to know the same.

Jesus served others and gave his life for the lost; we can do likewise.

Jesus dealt with anxiety about death; you can too.

God's desire, his plan, his ultimate goal is to make you into the image of Christ.

—*EVERY DAY DESERVES A CHANCE*

Heavenly Father, thank you for shaping our lives to be like your Son, Jesus. May we become more like him each minute and hour of the day. As he had no bad habits, Father, do away with ours. As he served others, may we do the same. He faced fears with courage, and this is what we long to do. Weave the threads of our lives, Father, in such a way that the final tapestry will show the true image of Christ, amen.

But we all, with unveiled faces, beholding as in a mirror the glory of the Lord, are being transformed into the same image from glory to glory, just as by the Spirit of the Lord.

2 Corinthians 3:18

But now. O Lord,

You are our Father;

We are the clay, and You our potter;

And all we are the work of Your hand.

Isaiah 64:8

*"Let me teach you, because I am humble and gentle at heart,
and you will find rest for your souls."*

MATTHEW 11:29 NLT

LOVE THAT VALUES EVERY CREATURE

When Jesus says, "You are worth more than many sparrows" (Matthew 10:31 NIV), trust him. He knows. He knows the value of every creature.

When Christ declares, "Your Father knows what you need before you ask Him" (Matthew 6:8 NASB), believe it. After all, "He was in the beginning with God" (John 1:2 NASB).

Jesus claims to be not a top theologian, an accomplished theologian, or even the Supreme Theologian, but rather the Only Theologian. "No one really knows the Father except the Son." He does not say, "No one really knows the Father like the Son" or "in the fashion of the Son." But rather, "No one really knows the Father except the Son."

Heaven's door has one key, and Jesus holds it. . . .

Jesus knows the dimensions of God's throne room, the fragrance of its incense, the favorite songs of the unceasing choir. He has a unique, one-of-a-kind, unrivaled knowledge of God and wants to share his knowledge with you. "No one really knows the Father except the Son and those to whom the Son chooses to reveal him" (Matthew 11:27 NLT).

Jesus doesn't boast in his knowledge; he shares it. He doesn't gloat; he gives. He doesn't revel; he reveals. He reveals to us the secrets of eternity.

And he shares them, not just with the top brass or purebred, but with the hungry and needy. In the very next line, Jesus invites: "Come to me, all of you who are weary and carry heavy burdens, and I will give you rest. Take my yoke upon you. Let me teach you, because I am humble and gentle at heart, and you will find rest for your souls" (vv. 28–29 NLT).

–3:16: The Numbers of Hope

Blessed Savior, it is a joy to be reminded of your divine knowledge. No matter what problems are perplexing to us, we can bring them to you for solutions. You have the answers to our questions. We can rest assured that though the future is uncertain to us, it is well known to you. You care for the sparrows and you care even more for us, not just today but every day. Thank you for your love and your faithfulness, amen.

Consider the ravens, for they neither sow nor reap,
which have neither storehouse nor barn; and God feeds them.
Of how much more value are you than the birds?

Luke 12:24

"Handle Me and see, for a spirit does not have flesh and bones as you see I have."

LUKE 24:39

NO FEAR OF DEATH

More than five hundred eyewitnesses saw the resurrected Christ. They saw him physically.

They saw him factually. They didn't see a phantom or experience a sentiment. Grave eulogies often include such phrases as "She'll live on forever in my heart." Jesus' followers weren't saying this. They saw Jesus "in the flesh."

When he appeared to the disciples, he assured them, "It is I myself!" (Luke 24:39 NIV). The Emmaus-bound disciples saw nothing extraordinary about his body. His feet touched the ground. His hands touched the bread. They thought he was a fellow pilgrim until "their eyes were opened" (v. 31 NIV). Mary saw Jesus in the garden and called him "sir" (John 20:15 NIV). The disciples saw Jesus cooking fish on the shore. The resurrected Christ did physical deeds in a physical body. "I am not a ghost," he informed (Luke 24:39 NLT). "Handle Me and see, for a spirit does not have flesh and bones as you see I have" (v. 39).

Jesus experienced a physical and factual resurrection. And—here it is—because he did, we will too!

"Christ was raised as the first of the harvest; then all who belong to Christ will be raised when he comes back" (1 Corinthians 15:23 NLT). . . .

Death is not to be feared. . . . Your last moment is not your worst. . . . Five hundred witnesses left a still-resounding testimony: it's safe to die.

So let's die with faith. Let's allow the resurrection to sink into the fibers of our hearts and define the way we look at the grave. Let it "free those who were like slaves all their lives because of their fear of death" (Hebrews 2:15 NCV).

—*FEARLESS*

Loving Jesus, death is not something we need to fear. You have promised us eternal life with you. And your resurrection is a testimony to us that we too will rise again to live with you forever. You went to the grave and returned so we can do the same. This brings hope when we face the death of a loved one or our own death, amen.

Looking unto Jesus, the author and finisher of our faith.

HEBREWS 12:2

For the LORD God is a sun and shield; the LORD will give grace and glory; no good thing will He withhold from those who walk uprightly.

WORRY OR GOD'S WORD?

God says: "Every detail in our lives of love for God is worked into something good" (Romans 8:28 MSG).

Worry takes a look at catastrophes and groans, "It's all coming unraveled."

God's Word says, "[God has] done it all and done it well" (Mark 7:37 MSG).

Worry disagrees: "The world has gone crazy."

God's Word calls God "the blessed controller of all things" (1 Timothy 6:15 PHILLIPS).

Worry wonders if anyone is in control.

God's Word declares, "God will take care of everything you need" (Philippians 4:19 MSG).

Worry whispers this lie: "God doesn't know what you need."

God's Word reasons: "You're at least decent to your own children. So don't you think the God who conceived you in love will be even better?" (Matthew 7:11 MSG).

Worry discounts and replies, "You're on your own. It's you against the world."

Worry wages war on your faith.

—*EVERY DAY DESERVES A CHANCE*

O Lord, your Word declares your power to provide and your might to move on our behalf. When it seems like the world has gone crazy, your Word assures that you are still in control. You know our needs even before we do. You are working every little detail in our lives into something good. So rather than look at the chaos and confusion of life with an attitude of worry and doubt, we honor you with an attitude of firm faith. We will face the future with confidence and peace, amen.

"These things I have spoken to you, that My joy
may remain in you, and that your joy may be full."

JOHN 15:11

My brethren, count it all joy when you fall into various trials,
knowing that the testing of your faith produces patience.

JAMES 1:2–3

He has put a new song in my mouth—praise to our God.

PSALM 40:3

I will praise You, for I am fearfully and wonderfully made; marvelous are Your works, and that my soul, knows very well.

PSALM 139:14

YOU ARE GOD'S IDEA

Fashion designers tell us, "You'll be somebody if you wear our jeans. Stick our name on your rear end, and insignificance will vanish." So we do. And for a while . . . fashion redeems us from the world of littleness and nothingness, and we are something else.

Why? Because we spent half a paycheck on a pair of Italian jeans.

But then, horror of horrors, the styles change, the fad passes, the trend shifts from tight to baggy, faded to dark, and we're left wearing yesterday's jeans, feeling like yesterday's news.

Fear of insignificance creates the result it dreads, arrives at the destination it tries to avoid, facilitates the scenario it disdains. If a basketball player stands at the foul line repeating, "I'll never make the shot, I'll never make the shot," guess what? He'll never make the shot. If you pass your days mumbling, "I'll never make a difference; I'm not worth anything," guess what? You will be sentencing yourself to a life of gloom without parole.

Even more, you are disagreeing with God. Questioning his judgment. Second-guessing his taste.

According to him you were "skillfully wrought" (Psalm 139:15). You were "fearfully and wonderfully made" (v. 14). He can't stop thinking about you! If you could count his thoughts of you, "they would be more in number than the sand" (v. 18).

Why does he love you so much? The same reason the artist loves his paintings or the boat builder loves his vessels. You are his idea. And God has only good ideas. "For we are God's masterpiece. He has created us anew in Christ Jesus, so we can do the good things he planned for us long ago" (Ephesians 2:10 NLT).

—*FEARLESS*

Thank you, Father, that we are your masterpieces. You sculpted us from nothing into something. Thank you for the careful details you poured into creating our lives. Your thoughts about your children are more than the sands of the sea, and you have engraved our names on the palm of your hand. May we never make the foolish mistake of thinking we are not significant by worldly standards. We belong to you, amen.

Everyone who is called by My name, whom I have created for My glory; I have formed him, yes. I have made him.

ISAIAH 43:7

Loved with a Merciful Love

*If we confess our sins, He is faithful and just to forgive us
our sins and to cleanse us from all unrighteousness.*

1 JOHN 1:9

LOVED WITH A MERCIFUL LOVE

"God's well of grace must have a bottom to it," we rea-son. "A person can request forgiveness only so many times," contends our common sense. "Cash in too many mercy checks, and sooner or later one is going to bounce!" The devil loves this line of logic. If he can con-vince us that God's grace has limited funds, we'll draw the logical conclusion. The account is empty. God has locked the door to his throne room. Pound all you want; pray all you want. No access to God.

"No access to God" unleashes a beehive of con-cerns. We are orphans, unprotected and exposed. Heaven, if there is such a place, has been removed from the itinerary. Vulnerable in this life and doomed in the next. The fear of disappointing God has teeth. . . .

Nothing fosters fear like an ignorance of mercy. May I speak candidly? If you haven't accepted God's forgive-ness, you are doomed to fear. Nothing can deliver you from the gnawing realization that you have disregarded your Maker and disobeyed his instruction. No pill, pep talk, psychiatrist, or possession can set the sinner's heart at ease. You may deaden the fear, but you can't remove it. Only God's grace can.

Have you accepted the forgiveness of Christ? If not, do so. "If we confess our sins, He is faithful and just to forgive us our sins and to cleanse us from all unrighteousness" (1 John 1:9). Your prayer can be as simple as this: *Dear Father, I need forgiveness. I admit that I have turned away from you. Please forgive me. I place my soul in your hands and my trust in your grace. Through Jesus I pray, amen.*

Having received God's forgiveness, live forgiven! . . . When Jesus sets you free, you are free indeed.

—*Fearless*

How amazing, precious Lord, is your forgiveness. No matter how many times we fail, we will confess our sin and accept your faithful mercy. Lord, you are always listening to our prayers, and there is no limit to your amazing power. Your love never quits or gives up. We awaken each day to your magnificent love, amen.

I will glorify Your name forevermore.
For great is Your mercy toward me.

Psalm 86:12–13

I will praise You, for You have . . . become my salvation.

Psalm 118:21

The LORD's love never ends; his mercies never stop.
They are new every morning.

LAMENTATIONS 3:22—23 NCV

NEW EVERY MORNING

You messed up yesterday. You said the wrong words, took the wrong turn, loved the wrong person, reacted the wrong way. You spoke when you should have listened, walked when you should have waited, judged when you should have trusted, indulged when you should have resisted.

You messed up yesterday. But you'll mess up more if you let yesterday's mistakes sabotage today's attitude. God's mercies are new every morning. Receive them. Learn a lesson from the Cascade forests of Washington State. Some of its trees are hundreds of years old, far surpassing the typical life span of fifty to sixty years. One leaf-laden patriarch dates back seven centuries! What makes the difference? Daily drenching rains. Deluges keep the ground moist, the trees wet, and the lightning impotent.[18]

Lightning strikes you as well. Thunderbolts of regret can ignite and consume you. Counteract them with downpours of God's grace, daily washings of forgiveness. Once a year won't do. Once a month is insufficient. Weekly showers leave you dry. Sporadic mistings leave you combustible. You need a solid soaking every day. "The LORD's love never ends; his mercies never stop. They are new every morning" (Lamentations 3:22–23 NCV).

—*EVERY DAY DESERVES A CHANCE*

Mighty God, your loyal love is our hope. When we mess up, your tender kindness covers us with acceptance and forgiveness. No matter how often we disappoint you, we can trust ourselves to your mercy and know we will find your love. You will never turn away from us when we fail. You set our feet back on the right path and guide us in the way to go. We need a solid soaking of your grace and mercy every day, amen.

Praise the LORD! . . . for His merciful kindness is great toward us.

PSALM 117:1–2

My soul shall be joyful in my God; for He has clothed me with the garments of salvation.

ISAIAH 61:10

Salvation belongs to the LORD. Your blessing is upon your people.

PSALM 3:8

*"I—yes, I alone—am the one who blots out your sins for
my own sake and will never think of them again."*

ISAIAH 43:25 NLT

THE WORK IS FINISHED

Grace offers rest. Legalism never does. Then why do we
embrace it? "Those who trust in themselves are foolish"
(Proverbs 28:26 NCV). Why do we trust in ourselves? Why
do we add to God's finished work? Might the answer
include the verb *boast*?

Saving yourself is heady stuff. Even headier than a
high school varsity football jacket. I still own mine. I
wore it every day of my senior year. Who cared if the
temperature was in the nineties? I wanted everyone to
see what I had accomplished. If making a football team
feels great, how much more would earning a spot on
God's team?

But the truth is, we don't. If we think we do, we
have missed the message. "What is left for us to brag
about?" Paul wonders (Romans 3:27 CEV). What is there
indeed? What have you contributed? Aside from your
admission of utter decadence, I can't think of a thing.
"By His doing you are in Christ Jesus" (1 Corinthians
1:30 NASB). Salvation glorifies the Savior, not the saved.

Your salvation showcases God's mercy. It makes
nothing of your effort but everything of his. "I—yes, I

alone—am the one who blots out your sins *for my own sake* and will never think of them again" (Isaiah 43:25 NLT). . . .

Can you add anything to this salvation? No. The work is finished.

–IT'S NOT ABOUT ME

Father God, forgive us when we trust in ourselves for salvation rather than in the finished work of Christ. May we cherish the gift of salvation through the death of your Son, Jesus Christ. When we feel the urge to earn your love, remind us again of your never-ending, great, and generous grace. Remind us that the work is finished, amen.

I have trusted in Your mercy;
my heart shall rejoice in Your salvation.

PSALM 13:5

All the ends of the earth have seen the salvation
of our God. Shout joyfully to the LORD.

PSALM 98:3–4

Don't insist on getting even; that's not for you to do.
"I'll do the judging," says God. "I'll take care of it."
ROMANS 12:19 MSG

GOD DISPENSES PERFECT JUSTICE

Your enemies still figure into God's plan. Their pulse is proof: God hasn't given up on them. They may be out of God's will, but not out of his reach. You honor God when you see them not as his failures, but as his projects.

Besides, who assigned us the task of vengeance? . . .

God occupies the only seat on the supreme court of heaven. He wears the robe and refuses to share the gavel. For this reason Paul wrote, "Don't insist on getting even; that's not for you to do. 'I'll do the judging,' says God. 'I'll take care of it'" (Romans 12:19 MSG).

Revenge removes God from the equation. Vigilantes displace and replace God. "I'm not sure you can handle this one, Lord. You may punish too little or too slowly. I'll take this matter into my hands, thank you."

Is this what you want to say? Jesus didn't. No one had a clearer sense of right and wrong than the perfect Son of God. Yet, "when he suffered, he didn't make any threats but left everything to the one who judges fairly" (1 Peter 2:23 GOD'S WORD).

Only God assesses accurate judgments. We impose punishments too slight or severe. God dispenses perfect justice. Vengeance is his job. Leave your enemies in God's hands. You're not endorsing their misbehavior when you do. You can hate what someone did without letting hatred consume you.

—FACING YOUR GIANTS

Heavenly Father, you know the people who have hurt us. You know when the actions of other people have been unkind and unfair. When we want to get vengeance, Father, keep our hearts and minds focused on you. Help us understand that these people are still part of your plan. Remind us that you alone can accurately judge everyone and you alone dispense perfect justice. Teach us to turn thoughts of revenge into prayers of praise, amen.

"And will not God bring about justice for his chosen ones, who cry out to him day and night? . . . I tell you, he will see that they get justice, and quickly."

LUKE 18:7–8

God has chosen the foolish things of
the world to put to shame the wise.

1 CORINTHIANS 1:27

REMEMBER WHO HOLDS YOU

The act of conversion is a humbling one. We confess sins, beg for mercy, bend our knees. We let someone lower us into the waters of baptism. We begin as self-effacing souls. Timid children who extend muddy hands to our sinless God. We relate to the thief on the cross, identify with David's forgiven adultery, and find hope in Peter's forgiven betrayal. We challenge Paul's claim to the chief-of-sinners title, wondering if anyone could need or treasure grace as much as we do.

We come to God humbly. No swagger, no boasts, no "all by myself" declarations. We flex no muscles and claim no achievements. We cup sullied hearts in hands and offer them to God as we would a crushed, scentless flower: "Can you bring life to this?"

And he does. *He* does. We don't. He works the miracle of salvation. He immerses us in mercy. He stitches together our shredded souls. He deposits his Spirit and implants heavenly gifts. Our big God blesses our small faith.

We understand the roles. He is the Milky Way galaxy. We are the sand flea. He is U2, and we are the neighborhood garage band, and that's okay. We need a big God because we've made a big mess of our lives. Gradually our big God changes us. And, gratefully, we lust less, love more, lash out less, look heavenward more. We pay bills, pay attention to spouses, pay respect to parents. . . .

Take time to remember. "Look at what you were when God called you" (1 Corinthians 1:26 NCV). Remember who held you in the beginning. Remember who holds you today.

–Outlive Your Life

Loving Father, you work the miracle in salvation in our lives when we bow humbly before you. You immerse us in your mercy, and you fill our hearts with your Holy Spirit. Then you begin to change our lives to reflect your Son. You are a big God who brings big changes to our lives. We want to remember all you have done for us. You have given us truth to follow on the pathway of life and hope for an eternal future with you. May we never forget that you held us in the beginning and you hold us today, amen.

He received them and spoke to them about the kingdom of God, and healed those who had need of healing.

Luke 9:11

"Unless one is born again, he cannot see the kingdom of God."

JOHN 3:3

YOU MUST BE BORN AGAIN

The noisy room silences as Nicodemus enters. The men are wharf workers and tax collectors, unaccustomed to the highbrow world of a scholar. They shift in their seats. Jesus motions for the guest to sit. Nicodemus does and initiates the most famous conversation in the Bible: "Rabbi, we know that You are a teacher come from God; for no one can do these signs that You do unless God is with him" (John 3:2).

Nicodemus begins with what he "knows." *I've done my homework,* he implies. *Your work impresses me.*

We listen for a kindred salutation from Jesus: "And I've heard of you, Nicodemus." We expect, and Nicodemus expected, some hospitable chitchat.

None comes. Jesus makes no mention of Nicodemus's VIP status, good intentions, or academic credentials, not because they don't exist, but because, in Jesus' algorithm, they don't matter. He simply issues this proclamation: "Unless one is born again, he cannot see the kingdom of God" (v. 3).

Behold the Continental Divide of Scripture, the international date line of faith. Nicodemus stands on one side, Jesus on the other, and Christ pulls no punches about their differences.

Nicodemus inhabits a land of good efforts, sincere gestures, and hard work. Give God your best, his philosophy says, and God does the rest.

Jesus' response? Your best won't do. Your works don't work. Your finest efforts don't mean squat. Unless you are born again, you can't even see what God is up to.

−3:16: The Numbers of Hope

Thank you, Almighty God, for providing salvation for all who submit to you. We praise you that we can be born into your spiritual kingdom out of a life of sin. What a relief to know that we do not have to work to become your child; we simply accept the work of Jesus' death on the cross. Your offer of salvation is a marvelous miracle of mercy. It is a free gift from your generous heart given to all who don't deserve it but desperately need it. We praise you for your magnificent work, amen.

"Not everyone who says to me, 'Lord, Lord,' will enter the kingdom of heaven, but only those who do the will of my Father who is in heaven.".

Matthew 7:21 niv

The LORD your God. . . . He will rejoice over you with gladness, He will quiet you with His love, He will rejoice over you with singing.

GOD'S IMMEASURABLE LOVE

Several hundred feet beneath my chair is a lake, an underground cavern of crystalline water known as the Edwards Aquifer. We South Texans know much about this aquifer. We know its length (175 miles). We know its layout (west to east, except under San Antonio, where it runs north to south). We know the water is pure. Fresh. It irrigates farms and waters lawns and fills pools and quenches thirst. We know much about the aquifer.

But for all the facts we do know, there is an essential one we don't. We don't know its size. The depth of the cavern? A mystery. Number of gallons? Unmeasured. No one knows the amount of water the aquifer contains.

Watch the nightly weather report, and you'd think otherwise. Meteorologists give regular updates on the aquifer level. You get the impression that the amount of water is calculated. "The truth is," a friend told me, "no one knows how much water is down there."

Could this be? I decided to find out. I called a water conservationist. "That's right," he affirmed. "We esti-mate. We try to measure. But the exact quantity? No one knows." Remarkable. We use it, depend upon it, would perish without it . . . but measure it? We can't.

Bring to mind another unmeasured pool? It might. Not a pool of water but a pool of love. God's love. Aquifer fresh. Pure as April snow. One swallow slackens the thirsty throat and softens the crusty heart. Immerse a life in God's love, and watch it emerge cleansed and changed. We know the impact of God's love.

But the volume? No person has ever measured it.

–*It's Not About Me*

Your love, Father God, is without limit. We depend on it, but we can't begin to measure it. Your love rests on us like a holy blessing. From day to day and hour to hour, we enjoy the benefits of your faithful and eternal love. You paid the price for our salvation with the death of your Son. You accept us into your family as your children. You guide us and teach us your ways. You never leave us without your immeasurable love for one fraction of a second. You never quit showing us your tenderness and kindness. We rest joyfully in your hands, amen.

Behold what manner of love the Father has bestowed on us,
that we should be called children of God!

1 John 3:1

I come to you in the name of the LORD of hosts,
the God of the armies of Israel.

1 SAMUEL 17:45

LET'S MAJOR IN GOD

David just showed up this morning. He clocked out of sheep watching to deliver bread and cheese to his brothers on the battlefront. That's where David hears Goliath defying God. . . .

Read the first words he spoke, not just in the battle, but in the Bible: "David asked the men standing near him, 'What will be done for the man who kills this Philistine and removes this disgrace from Israel? Who is this uncircumcised Philistine that he should defy the armies of the living God?'" (1 Samuel 17:26 NIV).

David shows up discussing God. The soldiers mentioned nothing about him, the brothers never spoke his name, but David takes one step onto the stage and raises the subject of the living God. . . .

No one else discusses God. David discusses no one else but God. . . .

David sees what others don't and refuses to see what others do. All eyes, except David's, fall on the brutal, hate-breathing hulk. . . . The people know his taunts, demands, size, and strut. They have majored in Goliath.

David majors in God. He sees the giant, mind you;

he just sees God more so. Look carefully at David's battle cry: "You come to me with a sword, with a spear, and with a javelin. But I come to you in the name of the LORD of hosts, the God of the armies of Israel" (1 Samuel 17:45).

—FACING YOUR GIANTS

Lord God, train us to walk on your path. Teach us to see you in situations that are dangerous and difficult. Like David, when we are surrounded by overwhelming challenges, may our thoughts and words turn first to you. Rather than discuss the problem, remind us to discuss you. May our first thought in the morning and our last thought at night be centered on you. Rather than worry about the impossibilities, let us major in your mighty power. When we are tempted to look at the giants in our lives, we will choose to look at you, amen.

Let the God of my salvation be exalted!

PSALM 18:46

We walk by faith, not by sight.

2 CORINTHIANS 5:7

Cheerfully share your home with those
who need a meal or a place to stay.

1 Peter 4:9 nlt

Reach Out to People

In one of Jesus' resurrection appearances, he accompanies two disciples as they walk from Jerusalem to their village of Emmaus. The trail is a seven-mile journey, the better part of a day's walk for grown, healthy men. They converse the entire trip. Jesus gives them an overview of the Bible, beginning with the teachings of Moses right up to the events of their day. Still, they don't recognize him.

As they near their village, Jesus acts as if he is going to continue on his journey. We aren't told how he sent this message. Maybe he pulled out his pocket calendar and mumbled something about an evening appointment in the next town. We don't know how he left the impression, but he did. The Emmaus-bound disciples had another idea. "But they urged him strongly, 'Stay with us, for it is nearly evening; the day is almost over'" (Luke 24:29 niv).

It had been a long day. The two pilgrims had much on their mind. Certainly they had obligations and people in their lives. But their fellow traveler stirred a fire in their hearts. So they welcomed him in. Still not knowing that their guest was Jesus, they pulled out an extra chair, poured some water in the soup, and offered bread. Jesus blessed the bread, and when he did, "their eyes were opened and they recognized him" (v. 31 NIV).

We still encounter people on the road. And sometimes we sense a peculiar warmth, an affection. We detect an urge to open our doors to them. In these moments, let's heed the inner voice. We never know whom we may be hosting for dinner.

–OUTLIVE YOUR LIFE

Dear Lord Jesus, you spent your life here on earth caring for others. You reached out to the hopeless and the hurting with compassion. You forgave those who insulted you and tried to destroy you. Seeking hearts found answers from you. Weary hearts found rest. You lifted up those who were beat down by life. Your kind heart broke for the entire world. May we follow your example and spend our lives reaching out to others. When we are tempted to turn away from people, let us show them your love instead, amen.

As the elect of God . . . put on tender mercies, kindness, humility, meekness, longsuffering, bearing with one another.

COLOSSIANS 3:12–13

He was transfigured before them. His face shone like the sun,
and His clothes became as white as the light.

MATTHEW 17:2

LOVED BY A POWERFUL GOD

Light spilled out of him. Brilliant. Explosive. Shocking. Brightness poured through every pore of his skin and stitch of his robe. Jesus on fire. To look at his face was to look squarely into Alpha Centauri. Mark wants us to know that Jesus' "clothes shimmered, glistening white, whiter than any bleach could make them" (Mark 9:3 MSG).

This radiance was not the work of a laundry; it was the presence of God.

How long since . . . a fresh understanding of Christ buckled your knees and emptied your lungs? Since a glimpse of him left you speechless and breathless? If it's been a while, that explains your fears.

When Christ is great, our fears are not.

As awe of Jesus expands, fears of life diminish. A big God translates into big courage. A small view of God generates no courage. A limp, puny, fireless Jesus has no power over cancer cells, corruption, identity theft, stock-market crashes, or global calamity. A packageable, portable Jesus might fit well in a purse or on a shelf, but he does nothing for your fears.

Don't we need to know the transfigured Christ? One who spits holy fires? Who convenes and commands historical figures? Who occupies the loftiest perch and wears the only true crown of the universe, God's beloved Son? . . .

The longer we live in him, the greater he becomes in us. It's not that he changes but that we do; we see more of him. We see dimensions, aspects, and characteristics we never saw before, increasing and astonishing increments of his purity, power, and uniqueness. . . .

In the end we . . . fall on our faces and worship. And when we do, the hand of the carpenter extends through the tongue of towering fire and touches us. "Arise, and do not be afraid" (Matthew 17:7).

—FEARLESS

Almighty God, we worship and praise you for your mighty and glorious power. We stand in awe of you, the true king of the universe. We bow before the radiance of your holiness and purity. We rest humbly in your presence. This is where we find peace and rest and the right perspective on all that happens in life. Knowing you and living for you is the joy of my life. Thank you for your goodness and grace. This is truly good news, amen.

The LORD is great and greatly to be praised.

PSALM 96:4

Forever, O LORD, Your word is settled in heaven.

PSALM 119:89

UNCHANGING TRUTH

God's truth never wavers.

Would that we could say the same. We've learned to season our words with salt, we eat them so often. Our opinions change like Rodeo Drive fashion trends. (Weren't your convictions about child rearing stronger before you had kids? Do you know any Republicans who used to be Democrats and vice versa?) Our convictions tend to change.

Good to know God's don't. His view of right and wrong is the same with you and me as it was with Adam and Eve. "The word of our God shall stand for ever" (Isaiah 40:8 KJV). "For ever, O LORD, thy word is settled in heaven. . . . All thy commandments are truth. . . . Thou hast founded them for ever" (Psalm 119:89, 151–152 KJV).

Your outlook may change. My convictions may sway, but "the Scripture cannot be broken" (John 10:35). And since it can't, since his truth will not waver, God's ways will never alter.

He will always hate sin and love sinners, despise the proud and exalt the humble. He will always convict the evildoer and comfort the heavyhearted. He never changes direction midstream, recalibrates the course midway home, or amends the heavenly Constitution.

—*It's Not About Me*

Blessed Father, your words are the light we need to see how to walk on the path of life. Your words are a place of quiet retreat where we find rest and renewal. Your words are permanent and unchanging. Your truth is always the same; it is eternally right. We can rely on it and trust it as the pattern for our convictions and our decisions. Thank you for giving us this firm foundation for our faith, amen.

"For I am the LORD, I do not change;
Therefore you are not consumed, . . ."

MALACHI 3:6

The eternal God is your refuge,
And underneath are the everlasting arms; . . .

DEUTERONOMY 33:27

Let us therefore come boldly to the throne of grace, that we may obtain mercy and find grace to help in time of need.

HEBREWS 4:16

GOD MEETS DAILY NEEDS DAILY

You hate to worry. But what can you do to stop it? These three worry stoppers deserve your consideration:

Pray more. No one can pray and worry at the same time. When we worry, we aren't praying. When we pray, we aren't worrying. "You will keep him in perfect peace, whose mind is stayed on You, because he trusts in You" (Isaiah 26:3).

When you pray, you "stay" your mind on Christ, resulting in peace. Bow your knees and banish anxiety.

Want less. Most anxiety stems not from what we need, but from what we want.

"Delight yourselves in the Lord, yes, find your joy in him at all times" (Philippians 4:4 PHILLIPS). If God is enough for you, then you'll always have enough, because you'll always have God.

Live for today. Don't sacrifice it on the altar of anxiety.

God sends help at the hour we need it.

You don't have wisdom for tomorrow's problems. But you will tomorrow. You don't have resources for tomorrow's needs. But you will tomorrow. You don't have courage for tomorrow's challenges. But you will when tomorrow comes.

God meets daily needs daily and miraculously.

—<small>EVERY DAY DESERVES A CHANCE</small>

O Lord, you provide the answers and solutions for our questions and our problems. Steady our steps on the path of life. When we feel overwhelmed with worry, remind us to stop and pray. Let us choose to align ourselves with your plan for our lives rather than dwell on the problems. Remind us to live for today and trust you to give us the wisdom and resources for tomorrow when tomorrow comes. Thank you for meeting our needs each day in a truly miraculous way, amen.

"I am leaving you with a gift—peace of mind and heart. And the peace I give is a gift the world cannot give. So don't be troubled or afraid."

<small>JOHN 14:27 NLT</small>

The effective, fervent prayer of a righteous man avails much.

JAMES 5:16

PASSIONATE PRAYERS MOVE GOD'S HEART

When the problem is bigger than we are—we pray! "But while Peter was in prison, the church prayed very earnestly for him" (Acts 12:5 NLT).

They didn't picket the prison, petition the government, protest the arrest, or prepare for Peter's funeral. They prayed. They prayed as if prayer was their only hope, for indeed it was. They prayed "very earnestly for him."

One of our Brazilian church leaders taught me something about earnest prayer. He met Christ during a yearlong stay in a drug-rehab center. His therapy included three one-hour sessions of prayer a day. Patients weren't required to pray, but they were required to attend the prayer meeting. Dozens of recovering drug addicts spent sixty uninterrupted minutes on their knees.

I expressed amazement and confessed that my prayers were short and formal. He invited (dared?) me to meet him for prayer. I did the next day. We knelt on the concrete floor of our small church auditorium and began to talk to God. Change that. I talked; he cried, wailed, begged, cajoled, and pleaded. He pounded his fists on the floor, shook a fist toward heaven, confessed, and reconfessed every sin. He recited every promise in the Bible as if God needed a reminder.

Our passionate prayers move the heart of God. "The effective, fervent prayer of a righteous man avails much" (James 5:16). Prayer does not change God's nature; who he is will never be altered. Prayer does, however, impact the flow of history. God has wired his world for power, but he calls on us to flip the switch.

–Outlive Your Life

Lord Jesus, hardly a day arrives that doesn't bring problems that are bigger than us. Yet what seems impossible and overwhelming and frightening to us does not trouble you at all. Instead of carrying burdens we were never meant to carry, may we come to you in prayer and leave them at your feet. You hear our prayers and you promise to answer our prayers. You were faithful to us yesterday; you will still be faithful tomorrow. We praise you and call out to you with earnest hearts, amen.

The eyes of the Lord are on the righteous,
and His ears are open to their prayers.

1 Peter 3:12

You are my God; hear the voice of my supplications, O Lord.

Psalm 140:6

"I will ask the Father, and he will give you another Counselor to be with you forever."

John 14:16 NIV

Peace of Mind and Heart

The way we panic at the sight of change, you'd think bombs were falling on Iowa.

"Run for your lives! Graduation is coming!"

"The board of directors just hired a new CEO. Take cover!"

"Load the women and children into the bus, and head north. The department store is going out of business!"

Change trampolines our lives, and when it does, God sends someone special to stabilize us. On the eve of his death, Jesus gave his followers this promise: "When the Father sends the Advocate as my representative—that is, the Holy Spirit—he will teach you everything and will remind you of everything I have told you. I am leaving you with a gift—peace of mind and heart. And the peace I give is a gift the world cannot give. So don't be troubled or afraid" (John 14:26–27 NLT).

As a departing teacher might introduce the classroom to her replacement, so Jesus introduces us to the Holy Spirit. And what a ringing endorsement he gives. Jesus calls the Holy Spirit his "representative." The

Spirit comes in the name of Christ, with equal authority and identical power. Earlier in the evening Jesus had said, "I will ask the Father, and he will give you *another Counselor* to be with you forever" (John 14:16 NIV).

"Another Counselor." Both words shimmer. The Greek language enjoys two distinct words for *another*. One means "totally different," and the second translates "another just like the first one." When Jesus promises "another Counselor," he uses word number two, promising "another just like the first one."

And who is the first one? Jesus himself.

—*FEARLESS*

O Lord, you know every thought of our hearts. You know how easily we are frightened by change. But you have not left us to face change alone. You have given us a helper: your precious Holy Spirit. When life brings change and uncertainty and we start to panic, may the power of the Holy Spirit bring peace to our minds and hearts. May we honor you by replacing fear with trust, amen.

When He, the Spirit of truth, has come,
He will guide you into all truth. . . .

JOHN 16:13

He didn't love in order to get something from
us but to give everything of himself to us.
EPHESIANS 5:2 MSG

LOVED WITH AN INCOMPARABLE LOVE

Gomer was . . . an irascible woman married to a remarkable Hosea. She had the fidelity code of a prairie
jackrabbit, flirting and hopping from one lover to another. She ruined her life and shattered Hosea's heart.
Destitute, she was placed for sale in a slave market. Guess
who stepped forward to buy her? Hosea, who'd never
removed his wedding band. The way he treated her, you
would have thought she'd never loved another man. God
uses this story, indeed orchestrated this drama, to illustrate his steadfast love for his fickle people. . . .

His is agape love. Less an affection, more a decision;
less a feeling, more an action. . . .

Our finest love is a preschool watercolor to God's
Rembrandt, a vacant-lot dandelion next to his garden
rose. His love stands sequoia strong; our best attempts
bend like weeping willows.

Compare our love with God's? Look at the round
belly of the pregnant peasant girl in Bethlehem. God's
in there; the same God who can balance the universe on
the tip of his finger floats in Mary's womb. Why? Love.

Peek through the Nazareth workshop window. See

the lanky lad sweeping the sawdust from the floor? He once blew stardust into the night sky. Why swap the heavens for a carpentry shop? One answer: love.

Love explains why he came. Love explains how he endured.

His hometown kicked him out. A so-called friend turned him in. Hucksters called God a hypocrite. Sinners called God guilty. Do termites mock an eagle, tapeworms decry the beauty of a swan? How did Jesus endure such derision? . . . "Observe how Christ loved us. . . . He didn't love in order to get something from us but to give everything of himself to us" (Ephesians 5:2 MSG).

–3:16: THE NUMBERS OF HOPE

Blessed Savior, the thought of your strong love brings joy and hope. How grateful we are for your agape love that is steadfast and true. When we are discouraged by the fickle and feeble love of others, remind us of your totally unselfish love. May your extraordinary love be an example to us in loving others. May your generous love shape our lives, amen.

By this we know love, because He laid down His life for us.
And we also ought to lay down our lives for the brethren.

1 JOHN 3:16

"Father, forgive them, for they do not know what they do."
LUKE 23:34

UNDESERVED, UNEXPECTED GRACE

What does the thief on the cross next to Christ see? . . .
He sees the God who wrote the book on grace. The God
who coaxed Adam and Eve out of the bushes, murderous
Moses out of the desert. The God who made a place for
David, though David made a move on Bathsheba. The
God who didn't give up on Elijah, though Elijah gave up
on God. This is what the thief sees.

What does he hear? He hears what fugitive Moses
heard in the desert, depressed Elijah heard in the desert,
adulterous David heard after Bathsheba. He hears
what...

- a fickle Peter heard after the rooster crowed,
- the storm-tossed disciples heard after the wind stopped,
- the cheating woman heard after the men left,
- the oft-married Samaritan woman heard before the disciples came,
- the hardheaded and hard-hearted Saul would hear after the light shone,
- the paralytic heard when his friends lowered him through the roof,

- the blind man heard when Jesus found him on the street,
- the disciples would soon hear from Jesus on the beach early one morning.

He hears the official language of Christ: grace. Undeserved. Unexpected. Grace. "Today you will be with me in paradise" (Luke 23:43).

—*Every Day Deserves a Chance*

Precious Savior, we are amazed at your grace. You cancel out our sins and mistakes and restore us to a right relationship with our heavenly Father. You don't keep track of our sins. You wipe the slate clean with your mercy. Truly we are humbled by the gift of your grace. We don't deserve it, yet you freely give it. Even when we don't expect it, you offer it. We cannot make our hearts right. We trust you to do that for us. And we thank you for pouring your generous grace into our lives, amen.

Let us therefore come boldly to the throne of grace, that we may obtain mercy and find grace to help in time of need.

Hebrews 4:16

The LORD is near to all who call upon Him,
to all who call upon Him in truth.

PSALM 145:18

NEVER ALONE

Is God a distant deity? Mothers ask, "How can the presence of God come over my children?" Fathers ponder, "How can God's presence fill my house?" Churches desire the touching, helping, healing presence of God in their midst.

How can the presence of God come to us?

Should we light a candle, sing chants, build an altar, head up a committee, give a barrelful of money? What invokes the presence of God? . . .

God's present is his presence.

God's greatest gift is himself. Sunsets steal our breath. Caribbean blue stills our hearts. Newborn babies stir our tears. Lifelong love bejewels our lives. But take all these away—strip away the sunsets, oceans, cooing babies, and tender hearts—and leave us in the Sahara, and we still have reason to dance in the sand. Why? Because God is with us. . . .

God wants us to know. We are never alone. Ever.

God loves you too much to leave you alone, so he hasn't. He hasn't left you alone with your fears, your worries, your disease, or your death. So kick up your heels for joy. . . .

He is a personal God who loves and heals and helps and intervenes. He doesn't respond to magic potions or clever slogans. He looks for more. He looks for reverence, obedience, and God-hungry hearts.

And when he sees them, he comes!

–*FACING YOUR GIANTS*

Thank you, Lord God, that you are a personal God. You come right into our lives with help and healing. You do not stay far off from us, but you come up close. There is no place on earth so distant that we would not find you there. You love us too much to leave us alone. You care too much to let us face disease and death without you. Your generosity has filled our lives with an abundance of gifts: orchids, oceans, and cooing babies. But you are the greatest gift of all. We rejoice in you, amen.

My presence will go with you, and I will give you rest.

EXODUS 33:14

He who dwells in the secret place of the Most High
shall abide under the shadow of the Almighty.

PSALM 91:1

Our light affliction, which is but for a moment, is working
for us a far more exceeding and eternal weight of glory.

2 CORINTHIANS 4:17

"JUST FOR A MOMENT"

Remember the story of the eagle who was raised by chickens? From the floor of the barnyard, she spots an eagle in the clouds, and her heart stirs. "I can do that!" she whispers. The other chickens laugh, but she knows better. She was born different. Born with a belief.

You were too. Your world extends beyond the barnyard of time. A foreverness woos you. Your heavenly life Everests the pebbles of your earthly life. If grains of sand measured the two, how would they stack up? Heaven would be every grain of sand on every beach on earth, plus more. Earthly life, by contrast, would be one hundredth of one grain of sand. Need a phrase to summarize the length of your life on earth? Try: "Just a moment."

Wasn't this the phrase of choice for Paul? "Our light affliction, which is *but for a moment*, is working for us a far more exceeding and eternal weight of glory" (2 Corinthians 4:17).

What if we had a glimpse of the apostle as he wrote those words? By this time he had been "beaten times without number, often in danger of death. Five times," he writes, "I received from the Jews thirty-nine lashes. Three times I was beaten with rods, once I was stoned, three times I was shipwrecked, a night and a day I have spent in the deep" (2 Corinthians 11:23–25 NASB). He goes on to refer to life-threatening river trips, wilderness wanderings, and exposure to cold, attacks, hunger, and thirst. These, in Paul's words, are light afflictions to be endured for just a moment.

What if we took the same attitude toward life? What if we saw our tough times as a grain of sand scarcely worthy of contrast with the forever dunes?

–*It's Not About Me*

Lord Jesus, you have told us that we will have troubles and tribulation here on earth even as your children. But you have also promised to help us tackle these troubles. You promise your grace to overcome and your strength to triumphantly endure the hard times that come our way. When we face affliction, may we take Paul's view that it is just for a moment. May we keep a perspective that extends beyond the present problem to an eternity spent with you, amen.

When troubles come your way, consider it an opportunity for great joy. For you know that when your faith is tested, your endurance has a chance to grow. So let it grow, for when your endurance is fully developed, you will be perfect and complete, needing nothing.

JAMES 1:2–4 NLT

Be careful what you think, because your thoughts run your life.
PROVERBS 4:23 NCV

POSITIVE THOUGHTS PURVEY HOPE

Two types of voices command your attention today. Negative ones fill your mind with doubt, bitterness, and fear. Positive ones purvey hope and strength. Which ones will you choose to heed? You have a choice, you know. "We take every thought captive so that it is obedient to Christ" (2 Corinthians 10:5 GOD'S WORD).

Do you let anyone who knocks on your door enter your house? Don't let every thought that surfaces dwell in your mind. Take it captive . . . make it obey Jesus. If it refuses, don't think it.

Negative thoughts never strengthen you. How many times have you cleared a traffic jam with your grumbles? Does groaning about bills make them disappear? Why moan about your aches and pains, problems and tasks?

"Be careful what you think, because your thoughts run your life" (Proverbs 4:23 NCV).

—*EVERY DAY DESERVES A CHANCE*

O Lord, teach us to choose positive thoughts over negative thoughts. Help us take every thought captive, shape it to fit into a life that pleases you. May every emotion and impulse be pleasing to you. Rather than moan and groan about the difficult things in life, teach us to give up grumbling and be glad that you are in control of every detail. When we have the choice to fill our minds with doubt and bitterness or hope and strength, we will choose hope and strength, amen.

Set your mind on things above, not on things on the earth.

COLOSSIANS 3:2

Do not be conformed to this world, but be transformed by the renewing of your mind.

ROMANS 12:2

Comfort each other and edify one another, just as you also are doing.

Uncommon Comunity

Something holy happens around a dinner table that will never happen in a sanctuary. In a church auditorium you see the backs of heads. Around the table you see the expressions on faces. In the auditorium one person speaks; around the table everyone has a voice. Church services are on the clock. Around the table there is time to talk.

Hospitality opens the door to uncommon community.

It's no accident that *hospitality* and *hospital* come from the same Latin word, for they both lead to the same result: healing. When you open your door to someone, you are sending this message: "You matter to me and to God." You may think you are saying, "Come over for a visit." But what your guest hears is, "I'm worth the effort."

Do you know people who need this message? Singles who eat alone? Young couples who are far from home? Coworkers who've been transferred, teens who feel left out, and seniors who no longer drive? Some people pass an entire day with no meaningful contact with anyone else. Your hospitality can be their hospital.

You can join the ranks of people such as . . .

Abraham. He fed not just angels, but the Lord of angels (Genesis 18).

Rahab, the harlot. She received and protected the spies. Thanks to her kindness, her kindred survived, and her name is remembered (Joshua 6:22–23; Matthew 1:5).

Martha and Mary. They opened their home for Jesus. He, in turn, opened the grave of Lazarus for them (John 11:1–45; Luke 10:38–42).

–OUTLIVE YOUR LIFE

Lord Jesus, as you gave of yourself so generously to others, may we also look for ways to serve others. Let us use our time and talents and resources to help the hurting. Open our eyes to see people who are lonely and need a healing touch. Even if it may not always be convenient, teach us to open our hearts and homes to those who long for someone to be kind to them. Let us put the needs of others above our own self-serving interests. Let us be gracious examples of your love for the needy, amen.

They devoted themselves to the apostles' teachings and to the fellowship, to the breaking of the bread and to prayer.

ACTS 2:42 NIV

Because Jesus was raised from the dead, we've been given
a brand-new life and have everything to live for, including
a future in heaven—and the future starts now!

1 Peter 1:3–4 msg

HELP FOR YOUR CHALLENGES

Others offer life, but no one offers to do what Jesus does—to reconnect us to his power. But how can we know? How do we know that Jesus knows what he's talking about? The ultimate answer, according to his flagship followers, is the vacated tomb. Did you note the words you just read? "Because Jesus was raised from the dead, we've been given a brand-new life." In the final sum, it was the disrupted grave that convinced the maiden Christians to cast their lots with Christ. "He was seen by Peter and then by the twelve apostles. After that, Jesus was seen by more than five hundred of the believers at the same time" (1 Corinthians 15:5–6 ncv).

Can Jesus actually replace death with life? He did a convincing job with his own. We can trust him because he has been there. . . .

He's been to Bethlehem, wearing barn rags and hearing sheep crunch. Suckling milk and shivering against the cold. All of divinity content to cocoon itself in an eight-pound body and to sleep on a cow's supper. Millions who face the chill of empty pockets or the fears of sudden change turn to Christ. Why?

Because he's been there.

He's been to Nazareth, where he made deadlines and paid bills; to Galilee, where he recruited direct reports and separated fighters; to Jerusalem, where he stared down critics and stood up against cynics.

We have our Nazareths as well—demands and due dates. Jesus wasn't the last to build a team; accusers didn't disappear with Jerusalem's temple. Why seek Jesus' help with your challenges? Because he's been there.

—3:16: The Numbers of Hope

Precious Savior, you walked the dusty roads of Galilee. You lived in our world and experienced daily burdens and blessings just like we do. You set aside the robes of divinity to be wrapped in swaddling clothes. You know more about us and our world than we know ourselves. That is why we can come to you with complete assurance that you understand our empty pockets, our stressful demands, and our wounded hearts. We know that you are sympathetic to our every need, amen.

Thanks be to God who always leads us in triumph in Christ, and through us diffuses the fragrance of His knowledge in every place.

2 Corinthians 2:14

The LORD is on my side; I will not fear. What can man do to me?

PSALM 118:6

LOVED BY THE LORD OF LIFE

Satan cannot reach you without passing through God.

Then what are we to make of the occasions Satan does reach us? How are we supposed to understand the violence listed in Hebrews 11? . . . Or, most supremely, how are we to understand the suffering of Jesus? Ropes. Whips. Thorns. Nails. These trademarked his final moments. Do you hear the whip slapping against his back, ripping sinew from bone? . . .

In polite Roman society, the word *cross* was an obscenity, not to be uttered in conversation. Roman soldiers were exempt from crucifixion except in matters of treason. It was ugly and vile, harsh and degrading. And it was the manner by which Jesus chose to die. "He humbled himself and became obedient to death—even death on a cross!" (Philippians 2:8 NIV).

A calmer death would have sufficed. A single drop of blood could have redeemed humankind. Shed his blood, silence his breath, still his pulse, but be quick about it. Plunge a sword into his heart. Take a dagger to his neck. Did the atonement for sin demand six hours of violence?

No, but his triumph over sadism did. Jesus once and

for all displayed his authority over savagery. Evil may have her moments, but they will be brief. Satan unleashed his meanest demons on God's Son. He tortured every nerve ending and inflicted every misery. Yet the master of death could not destroy the Lord of life. Heaven's best took hell's worst and turned it into hope.

—*FEARLESS*

Lord of all the earth and heavens, we stand in awe to think how you suffered to bring salvation to your children. Because of your suffering, our sins are forgiven. You triumphed over evil and freed us from its tyranny. Your death brings hope and healing to our everyday lives. This greatest act of love gives grand gifts to all who will receive them. Thank you, amen.

We know that when He is revealed, we shall be like Him,
for we shall see Him as He is. And everyone who has
this hope in Him purifies himself, just as He is pure.

1 JOHN 3:2–3

Our soul waits for the LORD; He is our help and our shield. For our
heart shall rejoice in Him, because we have trusted in His holy name.

PSALM 33:20–21

My heart said to You, "Your face, LORD, I will seek."
PSALM 27:8

THE GLORY OF GOD

When Ezekiel saw it, he had to bow.

It encircled the angels and starstruck the shepherds in the Bethlehem pasture.

Jesus radiates it.

John beheld it.

Peter witnessed it on Transfiguration Hill.

Christ will return enthroned in it.

Heaven will be illuminated by it.

It gulfstreams the Atlantic of Scripture, touching every person with the potential of changing every life. Including yours. One glimpse, one taste, one sampling, and your faith will never be the same . . .

Glory.

God's glory.

To seek God's glory is to pray, "Thicken the air with your presence; make it misty with your majesty. Part heaven's drapes, and let your nature spill forth. God, show us God."

What the word *Alps* does for the mountains of Europe, *glory* does for God's nature. *Alps* encompasses a host of beauties: creeks, peaks, falling leaves, running elk. To ask to see the Alps is to ask to see it all. To ask to see God's glory is to ask to see all of God. God's glory carries the full weight of his attributes: his love, his character, his strength. . . .

Every act of heaven reveals God's glory. Every act of Jesus did the same.

—*It's Not About Me*

Father, we ask you to show us your glory. Open our eyes to behold your majesty and your powerful presence in our lives. May these glimpses of your glory change our lives forever. We want to keep our eyes on you as we try to live your holy best. We pray that every detail in our lives—words, actions, thoughts—would bring glory to you. Our goal is to bring honor to your glorious name. We celebrate you, amen.

They shall sing of the ways of the LORD,
for great is the glory of the LORD.

PSALM 138:5

Blessing and honor and glory and power be
to Him who sits on the throne.

REVELATION 5:13

We don't look at the troubles we can see now;
rather, we fix our gaze on things that cannot be seen.
2 CORINTHIANS 4:18 NLT

THE HAND OF THE WEAVER

Over a hundred years ago in England, the borough of West Stanley endured a great tragedy. A mine collapsed, trapping and killing many of the workers inside. The bishop of Durham, Dr. Handley Moule, was asked to bring a word of comfort to the mourners. Standing at the mouth of the mine, he said, "It is very difficult for us to understand why God should let such an awful disaster happen, but we know Him and we trust Him, and all will be right. I have at home," he continued, "an old bookmark given to me by my mother. It is worked in silk, and, when I examine the wrong side of it, I see nothing but a tangle of threads, crossed and re-crossed. It looks like a big mistake. One would think that someone had done it who did not know what she was doing. But, when I turn it over and look at the right side, I see there, beautifully embroidered, the letters GOD IS LOVE.

"We are looking at this today," he counseled, "from the wrong side. Someday we shall see it from another standpoint, and shall understand."[19]

Indeed we shall. Until then, focus less on the tangled threads and more on the hand of the weaver.

—EVERY DAY DESERVES A CHANCE

Loving God, our lives often seem to be a mass of tangled threads. Yet we know that you are the Master Weaver who is making something beautiful of our lives. When we are puzzled and perplexed and want to give up hope, encourage us to shape our worries into prayer. When our hearts waver, keep us steady. Teach us to replace our frazzled fears with confidence in you. Let our faith flourish, amen.

He is our God, and we are the people of His pasture,
and the sheep of His hand.

PSALM 95:7

Your faithfulness reaches to the clouds.
Your righteousness is like the great mountains.

PSALM 36:5–6

"I give them eternal life, and they shall never perish;
no one can snatch them out of my hand."

JOHN 10:28 NIV

GOD CARES FOR HIS CHILDREN

God takes start-to-finish-line responsibility for his children.

We parents understand God's resolve. When our children stumble, we do not disown them. When they fall, we do not dismiss them. We may punish or reprimand, but cast them out of the family? We cannot. They are biologically connected to us. Those born with our DNA will die with it.

God, our Father, engenders the same relationship with us. Upon salvation we "become children of God" (John 1:12 ESV). He alters our lineage, redefines our spiritual parenthood, and, in doing so, secures our salvation. To accomplish the mission, he seals us with his Spirit. "Having believed, you were marked in him with a seal, the promised Holy Spirit" (Ephesians 1:13 NIV). A soul sealed by God is safe.

For a short time in college, I worked at a vacuum cleaner plant. We assembled the appliance from plug to hose. The last step on the assembly line was "sealing and shipping." By this point, the company had invested hours and dollars in the machine. So they took extra care to protect their product. They mummified it in bubble wrap, secured it with Styrofoam, wrapped the box with tough-to-tear tape, stamped the destination on the box, and belted it inside the truck. That machine was secure. But compared to God's care of his saints, workers dumped bare machines into the back of a pickup truck. God vacuum-seals us with his strongest force: his Spirit. He sheathes his children in a suit of spiritual armor, encircles us with angels, and indwells us himself. The queen of England should enjoy such security.

Christ paid too high a price to leave us unguarded. "Remember, he has identified you as his own, guaranteeing that you will be saved on the day of redemption" (Ephesians 4:30 NLT). . . .

You may slip—indeed you will—but you will not fall.

—3:16: THE NUMBERS OF HOPE

God, my Father, it is an honor to be your child and to be sealed with your precious Holy Spirit. Thank you for securing our salvation and freeing us to rest peacefully in that security. Thank you for circling our lives with your angels and guarding us with your powerful love. You are the hope of our salvation, amen.

The Lord directs the steps of the godly. He
delights in every detail of their lives.

PSALM 37:23 NLT

"Why are you fearful, O you of little faith?"
MATTHEW 8:26

CONFIDENT IN GOD'S GOODNESS

"A great storm arose on the lake so that waves covered the boat, but Jesus was sleeping" (Matthew 8:24 NCV).

Now there's a scene. The disciples scream; Jesus dreams. Thunder roars; Jesus snores. He doesn't doze, catnap, or rest. He slumbers. His snooze troubles the disciples. Matthew and Mark record their responses as three staccato Greek pronouncements and one question.

The pronouncements: "Lord! Save! Dying!" (Matthew 8:25).

The question: "Teacher, do You not care that we are perishing?" (Mark 4:38).

They do not ask about Jesus' strength: "Can you still the storm?" His knowledge: "Are you aware of the storm?" Or his know-how: "Do you have any experience with storms?" But rather, they raise doubts about Jesus' character: "Do you not care . . . "

Fear does this. Fear corrodes our confidence in God's goodness. We begin to wonder if love lives in heaven. . . .

It also deadens our recall. The disciples had reason to trust Jesus. By now they'd seen him "healing all kinds of sickness and all kinds of disease among the people" (Matthew 4:23). They had witnessed him heal a leper with a touch and a servant with a command (8:3, 13). . . .

Do they remember the accomplishments of Christ? They may not. Fear creates a form of spiritual amnesia. It dulls our miracle memory. It makes us forget what Jesus has done and how good God is.

—*FEARLESS*

Gracious Lord, when the storms of life overwhelm us, open our eyes to see you in the midst of the storm. Enable us stay focused on you, not on people or circumstances. As you have so often in the past, replace the worry and terror with peace and hope. When we lose sight of your miracle-working power, remind us once again of all you have done and how good you are to your children, amen.

Happy is he who has the God of Jacob for his help,
whose hope is in the LORD his God.

PSALM 146:5

He gives power to the weak, and to those
who have no might He increases strength.

ISAIAH 40:29

Beholding as in a glass the glory of the Lord,
[we] are changed into the same image from
glory to glory, even as by the Spirit of the Lord.

2 CORINTHIANS 3:18 KJV

SON REFLECTORS

What does the moon do? She generates no light. Contrary to the lyrics of the song, this harvest moon cannot shine on. Apart from the sun, the moon is nothing more than a pitch-black, pockmarked rock. But properly positioned, the moon beams. Let her do what she was made to do, and a clod of dirt becomes a source of inspiration, yea, verily, romance. The moon reflects the greater light.

And she's happy to do so! You never hear the moon complaining. She makes no waves about making waves. Let the cow jump over her or astronauts step on her; she never objects. Even though sunning is accepted while mooning is the butt of bad jokes, you won't hear ol' Cheeseface grumble. The moon is at peace in her place. And because she is, soft light touches a dark earth.

What would happen if we accepted our place as Son reflectors?

Such a shift comes so stubbornly, however. We've been demanding our way and stamping our feet since infancy. Aren't we all born with a default drive set on self-ishness? *I want a spouse who makes me happy and coworkers who always ask my opinion. I want weather that suits me and traffic that helps me and a government that serves me. It is all about me. . . .*

How can we be bumped off self-center? . . . We move from me-focus to God-focus by pondering him. Witnessing him. Following the counsel of the apostle Paul: "Beholding as in a glass the glory of the Lord, [we] are changed into the same image from glory to glory, even as by the Spirit of the Lord" (2 Corinthians 3:18 KJV).

Beholding him changes us.

–*It's Not About Me*

O Lord, change our focus from a me-focus to a God-focus. Work your will in our lives that we might be instruments to do your work and to tell others of your great love. Let our lives reflect your holiness through thick and thin. Help us live in pursuit of what you want rather than what we want. May we keep a firm grip on our faith no matter what hard times come our way. In all we do, may we honor you, amen.

<hr>

Sing praise to the LORD . . . and give thanks
at the remembrance of His holy name.

PSALM 30:4

We have seen his glory, the glory of the One and Only,
who came from the Father, full of grace and truth.

JOHN 1:14 NIV

JESUS HAS ALL AUTHORITY

When parents beget or conceive a child, they transfer their DNA to the newborn. Jesus shares God's DNA. Jesus isn't begotten in the sense that he began but in the sense that he and God have the same essence, eternal life span, unending wisdom, and tireless energy. Every quality we attribute to God, we can attribute to Jesus.

"Anyone who has seen me has seen the Father!" Jesus claimed (John 14:9 NLT). And the epistle to the Hebrews concurs: "[Christ] is the radiance of [God's] glory and the exact representation of His nature" (1:3 NASB). . . .

Jesus claims not the most authority, but all authority. "My Father has entrusted everything to me" (Matthew 11:27 NLT).

Christ claims ultimate clout. Unshared supremacy. He steers the ship and pilots the plane. When he darts his eyes, oceans swell. When he clears his throat, birds migrate. He banishes bacteria with a single thought. "He sustains everything by the mighty power of his command" (Hebrews 1:3 NLT).

He is to history what a weaver is to a tapestry. I once watched a weaver work at a downtown San Antonio market. She selected threads from her bag and arranged them first on the frame, then on the shuttle. She next worked the shuttle back and forth over the threads, intertwining colors, overlapping textures. In a matter of moments a design appeared.

Christ, in like manner, weaves his story. Every person is a thread, every moment a color, every era a pass of the shuttle. Jesus steadily interweaves the embroidery of humankind. "'My thoughts are nothing like your thoughts,' says the LORD. 'And my ways are far beyond anything you could imagine'" (Isaiah 55:8 NLT).

−3:16: *THE NUMBERS OF HOPE*

Lord Jesus, you are the Master Weaver. You are carefully weaving each thread in our lives according to your perfect plan. Even when we cannot understand everything that is happening, we will trust you. Your thoughts are far beyond our thoughts. Thank you for the wisdom and love you are pouring into the story of our lives, amen.

Thank you for making me so wonderfully complex!
Your workmanship is marvelous—how well I know it.
You watched me as I was being formed in utter seclusion,
as I was being woven together in the dark of the womb.

PSALM 139:14–15 NLT

This is the day the LORD has made; we will rejoice and be glad in it.

GOD MADE THIS DAY

What of those days of double shadows? Those days when hope is Hindenburged by crisis? You never leave the hospital bed or wheelchair. You wake up and bed down in the same prison cell or war zone. The cemetery dirt is still fresh, the pink slip still folded in your pocket, the other side of the bed still empty . . . who has a good day on these days?

Most don't . . . but couldn't we try? Such days warrant an opportunity. A shot. A tryout. An audition. A swing at the plate. Doesn't every day deserve a chance to be a good day?

After all, "this is the day the LORD has made; we will rejoice and be glad in it" (Psalm 118:24). The first word in the verse leaves us scratching our heads. "*This* is the day the Lord has made"? Perhaps holidays are the days the Lord has made. Wedding days are the days the Lord has made. Easter Sundays . . . super-sale Saturdays . . . vacation days . . . the first days of hunting season—these are the days the Lord has made. But "*this* is the day"?

"This is the day" includes every day. Divorce days, final exam days, surgery days, tax days. Sending-your-firstborn-off-to-college days. . . .

God made this day, ordained this hard hour, designed the details of this wrenching moment. He isn't on holiday. He still holds the conductor's baton, sits in the cockpit, and occupies the universe's only throne. Each day emerges from God's drawing room. Including this one.

—*Every Day Deserves a Chance*

Father God, you have planned every day of our lives. This includes the sad days, the discouraging days, and the desperate days. When it is difficult for us to find good in our day, may we remember that each of our days emerges from your drawing room. You ordain every hour and the details of every day . . . even the hard ones. Increase our faith, Father. Help us to live deeply and surely in your unfailing love. Give us hearts to praise you even on the dark days, amen.

Sing, O heavens! Be joyful, O earth! . . .
For the Lord has comforted His people.

Isaiah 49:13

The Lord has been mindful of us; He will bless us.

Psalm 115:12

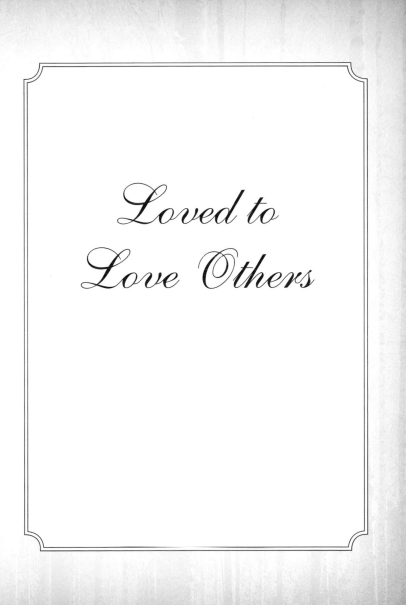

Loved to Love Others

"I was hungry, and you fed me. I was thirsty, and you gave me a drink."

MATTHEW 25:35 NLT

LOVED TO LOVE OTHERS

There are many reasons to help people in need. But for the Christian, none is higher than this: when we love those in need, we are loving Jesus. It is a mystery beyond science, a truth beyond statistics. But it is a message that Jesus made crystal clear: when we love them, we love him.

Many years ago I heard a woman discuss this work. She visited a Catholic church in downtown Miami, Florida, in 1979. The small sanctuary overflowed with people. I was surprised. . . . Some sat in windowsills. I found a spot against the back wall and waited. I don't know if the air-conditioning was broken or nonexistent, but the windows were open, and the south coast air was stuffy. The audience was chatty and restless. Yet when she entered the room, all stirring stopped. . . .

She wore her characteristic white Indian sari with a blue border that represented the Missionaries of Charity, the order she had founded in 1949. Her sixty-nine years had bent her already small frame. But there was nothing small about Mother Teresa's presence.

"Give me your unborn children," she offered. (Opening words or just the ones I remember most? I don't know.) "Don't abort them. If you cannot raise them, I will. They are precious to God."

Who would have ever pegged this slight Albanian woman as a change agent? Born in a cauldron of ethnic strife, the Balkans. Shy and introverted as a child. Of fragile health. One of three children. Daughter of a generous but unremarkable businessman. Yet somewhere along her journey, she became convinced that Jesus walked in the "distressing disguise of the poor," and she set out to love him by loving them. . . .

I wonder if God creates people like Mother Teresa so he can prove his point: "See, you can do something today that will outlive your life."

–OUTLIVE YOUR LIFE

Lord Jesus, help us outlive our lives for you. May our lives count for your kingdom. Let us be your hands, extended to those who need help. May we look for every opportunity to show your love to others. May your love be perfected in us as we give love gladly and freely. Open our hands to give gifts. Open our hearts to give kindness. Open our eyes to shed tears for the sorrows of others. Open our ears to hear hurting hearts, amen.

Let them do good, that they be rich in good works,
ready to give, willing to share.

1 TIMOTHY 6:18

"Let your light so shine before men, that they may see your good works and glorify your Father in heaven."

MATTHEW 5:16

DAILY DEEDS OF KINDNESS

In the final days of Jesus' life, he shared a meal with his friends Lazarus, Martha, and Mary. Within the week he would feel the sting of the Roman whip, the point of the thorny crown, and the iron of the executioner's nail. But on this evening, he felt the love of three friends.

For Mary, however, giving the dinner was not enough. "Mary came in with a jar of very expensive aromatic oils, anointed and massaged Jesus' feet, and then wiped them with her hair. The fragrance of the oils filled the house" (John 12:3 MSG). . . .

Judas criticized the deed as wasteful. Not Jesus. He received the gesture as an extravagant demonstration of love, a friend surrendering her most treasured gift. As Jesus hung on the cross, we wonder, *Did he detect the fragrance on his skin?*

Follow Mary's example.

There is an elderly man in your community who just lost his wife. An hour of your time would mean the world to him.

Some kids in your city have no dad. No father takes them to movies or baseball games. Maybe you can.

They can't pay you back. They can't even afford the popcorn or sodas. But they'll smile like a cantaloupe slice at your kindness.

Or how about this one? Down the hall from your bedroom is a person who shares your last name. Shock that person with kindness. Something outlandish. Your homework done with no complaints. Coffee served before he awakens. A love letter written to her for no special reason. Alabaster poured, just because.

Daily do a deed for which you cannot be repaid.

—EVERY DAY DESERVES A CHANCE

Precious Savior, we pass people every day who need a demonstration of your love. May we search for ways to show extravagant gestures of gracious love and outlandish acts of kindness. Make us people who set a goal of doing daily deeds for which we cannot be repaid. Set our hearts on fire for people who do not know you. Consume us with compassion for the desperate and downtrodden. Let us pour our lives out in love . . . just because, amen.

Since you have purified your souls in obeying the truth through the Spirit in sincere love of the brethren, love one another fervently with a pure heart, . . .

1 PETER 1:22

Resentment kills a fool, and envy slays the simple.
JOB 5:2 NIV

IMITATING GOD

Some people seem graced with mercy glands. They secrete forgiveness, never harboring grudges or reciting their hurts. Others of us (most of us?) find it hard to forgive the purveyors of pain in our lives.

We forgive the one-time offenders, mind you. We dismiss the parking place takers, date breakers, and even the purse snatchers. We can move past the misdemeanors, but the felonies? The repeat offenders? The ones who take our youth, retirement, or health?

Can you forgive the scum who hurt you?

Failure to do so could be fatal. "Resentment kills a fool, and envy slays the simple" (Job 5:2 NIV).

Vengeance fixes your attention at life's ugliest moments. Score-settling freezes your stare at cruel events in your past. Is this where you want to look? Will rehearsing and reliving your hurts make you a better person? By no means. It will destroy you.

I'm thinking of an old comedy routine. Joe complains to Jerry about the irritating habit of a mutual friend. The guy pokes his finger in Joe's chest as he talks. It drives Joe crazy. So he resolves to get even. He shows Jerry a small bottle of highly explosive nitroglycerin tied to a string. He explains, "I'm going to wear this around my neck, letting the bottle hang over the exact spot where I keep getting poked. Next time he sticks his finger in my chest, he'll pay for it."

Not nearly as much as Joe will, right? . . . An eye for an eye becomes a neck for a neck and a job for a job and a reputation for a reputation. When does it stop? It stops when one person imitates God.

—FACING YOUR GIANTS

Father God, it isn't easy to forgive those who hurt us. It is difficult not to harbor resentment and bitterness against them. But we know, Father, that harboring grudges is destructive. Give us the strength to lay all offenses at your feet, Father, and to leave them there. Help us imitate your matchless mercy and grace, amen.

"Whenever you stand praying, if you have anything against anyone, forgive him, that your Father in heaven may also forgive you your trespasses."

MARK 11:25

Love . . . bears all things, believes all things,
hopes all things, endures all things.

1 Corinthians 13:4, 7

Believe in Others

Everyone else has written off the person you care about. "He's too far gone." "She's too hard . . . too addicted . . . too old . . . too cold." No one gives a prayer. But you are beginning to realize that maybe God is at work behind the scenes. Maybe it's too soon to throw in the towel . . . You begin to believe.

Don't resist these thoughts.

Joseph didn't. His brothers sold him into Egyptian slavery. Yet he welcomed them into his palace.

David didn't. King Saul had a vendetta against David, but David had a soft spot for Saul. He called him "the Lord's anointed" (1 Samuel 24:10).

Hosea didn't. His wife, Gomer, was queen of the red-light district, but Hosea kept his front door open. And she came home.

Of course, no one believed in people more than Jesus did. He saw something in Peter worth developing, in the adulterous woman worth forgiving, and in John worth harnessing. He saw something in the thief on the cross, and what he saw was worth saving. And in the life of a wild-eyed, bloodthirsty extremist, he saw an apostle of grace. He believed in Saul.

Don't give up on your Saul. When others write him off, give him another chance. Stay strong. Call him brother. Call her sister. Tell your Saul about Jesus, and pray. And remember this: God never sends you where he hasn't already been. By the time you reach your Saul, who knows what you'll find.

—OUTLIVE YOUR LIFE

Thank you, Lord Jesus, that you believed in people. You looked beyond the mistakes and weaknesses to see potential and possibilities. No sinner was ever turned away from you. You opened your heart and your arms to the worst of the world when you gave your life on the cross. When people give up hope on themselves or others, open our eyes to see souls worth saving. Let us look beyond belligerence to see someone in need of your blessing. Let us look beyond pain and poverty to see someone saved by your mighty power, amen.

This is a faithful saying and worthy of all acceptance, that Christ Jesus came into the world to save sinners, of whom I am chief. However, for this reason I obtained mercy, that in me first Jesus Christ might show all longsuffering, as a pattern to those who are going to believe on Him for everlasting life.

1 TIMOTHY 1:15–16

Conduct your lives in love.
2 JOHN 6 MSG

THE GOD-CENTERED LIFE

Self-promotion. Self-preservation. Self-centeredness. It's all about me!

They all told us it was, didn't they? Weren't we urged to look out for number one? Find our place in the sun? Make a name for ourselves? We thought self-celebration would make us happy . . .

But what chaos this philosophy creates. What if a symphony orchestra followed such an approach? Can you imagine an orchestra with an "It's all about me" outlook? Each artist clamoring for self-expression. Tubas blasting nonstop. Percussionists pounding to get attention. The cellist shoving the flutist out of the center stage chair. The trumpeter standing atop the conductor's stool, tooting his horn. Sheet music disregarded. Conductor ignored. What do you have but an endless tune-up session!

Harmony? Hardly.

Happiness? Are the musicians happy to be in the group? Not at all. Who enjoys contributing to a cacophony?

You don't. We don't. We were not made to live this way. . . .

What would happen if we took our places and played our parts? If we played the music the Maestro gave us to play? If we made his song our highest priority?

Would we see a change in families? We'd certainly *hear* a change. Less "Here is what I want!" More "What do you suppose God wants?" . . .

Life makes sense when we accept our place. The gift of pleasures, the purpose of problems—all for him. The God-centered life works. And it rescues us from a life that doesn't.

–*It's Not About Me*

O Lord, rescue us from self-promotion and self-centeredness. Remind us that it is the God-centered life that works. Help us learn what part you want us to play in the orchestra of life, and give us the grace to make your song our highest priority. May we be willing to decrease so that you and your kingdom might increase. Give us godly hearts that serve you by serving others, amen.

If you try to hang onto your life, you will lose it. But if you give up your life for my sake and for the sake of the Good News, you will save it.

MARK 8:35 NLT

*Let each one of you in particular so love his own wife as himself,
and let the wife see that she respects her husband.*

EPHESIANS 5:33

YOUR MARRIAGE MASTERPIECE

Consider it your Testore cello. This finely constructed, seldom-seen instrument has reached the category of rare and is fast earning the status of priceless. Few musicians are privileged to play a Testore; even fewer are able to own one.

I happen to know a man who does. He, gulp, loaned it to me for a sermon. Wanting to illustrate the fragile sanctity of marriage, I asked him to place the nearly-three-centuries-old instrument on the stage, and I explained its worth to the church.

How do you think I treated the relic? Did I twirl it, flip it, and pluck the strings? No way. The cello is far too valuable for my clumsy fingers. Besides, its owner loaned it to me. I dared not dishonor his treasure.

On your wedding day, God loaned you his work of art: an intricately crafted, precisely formed masterpiece. He entrusted you with a one-of-a-kind creation. Value her. Honor him. Having been blessed with a Testore, why fiddle around with anyone else? . . .

Be fiercely loyal to one spouse. *Fiercely* loyal. Don't even look twice at someone else. No flirting. No teasing.

No loitering at her desk or lingering in his office. Who cares if you come across as rude or a prude? You've made a promise. Keep it. . . .

Make your wife the object of your highest devotion. Make your husband the recipient of your deepest passion. Love the one who wears your ring.

–*Facing Your Giants*

Father God, we dedicate our marriage to you. We ask that you would help us develop a relationship that pleases you in all ways. May we walk in step with each other and in step with your plans for our marriage. Help us to cultivate a sacrificial love for each other. May we love each other with diligence and consideration. Teach us to be gracious to each other and kind, setting aside all selfish interests for the good of the one who wears our ring. We want to give each other our highest devotion and our deepest passion. Most of all, we want our marriage to please you, amen.

"'For this reason a man will leave his father and mother and be united to his wife, and two will become one flesh'. . . . So they are no longer two, but one. Therefore what God has joined together, let man not separate."

Matthew 19:5–6 niv

"Whoever lives and believes in Me shall never die."
JOHN 11:26

GOD'S LOVING WELCOME

I love to hear my wife say "whoever." Sometimes I detect my favorite fragrance wafting from the kitchen: strawberry cake. I follow the smell like a bird dog follows a trail until I'm standing over the just-baked, just-iced pan of pure pleasure. Yet I've learned to still my fork until Denalyn gives clearance.

"Who is it for?" I ask.

She might break my heart. "It's for a birthday party, Max. Don't touch it!"

Or she might throw open the door of delight. "Whoever." And since I qualify as a "whoever," I say "yes."

Whoever. The pronoun is wonderfully indefinite. After all, who isn't a *whoever?*

The word sledgehammers racial fences and dynamites social classes. It bypasses gender borders and surpasses ancient traditions. *Whoever* makes it clear: God exports his grace worldwide. For those who attempt to restrict it, Jesus has a word: *Whoever.*

"*Whoever* acknowledges me before men, I will also acknowledge him before my Father in heaven" (Matthew 10:32 NIV).

"*Whoever* finds his life will lose it, and whoever

loses his life for my sake will find it" (Matthew 10:39 NIV).

"*Whoever* does God's will is my brother and sister and mother" (Mark 3:35 NIV).

"*Whoever* believes and is baptized will be saved, but whoever does not believe will be condemned" (Mark 16:16 NIV).

We lose much in life—sobriety, solvency, and sanity. We lose jobs and chances, and we lose at love. We lose youth and its vigor, idealism and its dreams. We lose much, but we never lose our place on God's "whoever" list.

Whoever—God's wonderful word of welcome.

−3:16: THE NUMBERS OF HOPE

Heavenly Father, your welcoming love is so refreshing. When there are so many qualifications and restrictions to love here on earth, your love for anyone and everyone is touches our hearts. We praise you for loving us enough to send your Son to die for us. May we take advantage of every opportunity to tell others about your welcoming love, especially those who feel left on the fringes of life, amen.

"Whoever acknowledges me before men, I will also acknowledge him before my Father in heaven."

MATTHEW 10:32 NIV

> *[God] comforts us in all our troubles so that we can comfort others. When they are troubled, we will be able to give them the same comfort God has given us.*
>
> 2 CORINTHIANS 1:4 NLT

CROSSING CULTURES, TOUCHING HEARTS

God loves the nations. He loves Iraqis. Somalians. Israelis. New Zealanders. Hondurans. He has a white-hot passion to harvest his children from every jungle, neighborhood, village, and slum. "*All the earth* shall be filled with the glory of the Lord" (Numbers 14:21 ESV). During the days of Joshua, God brought his people into Canaan "so that *all the peoples of the earth* may know that the hand of the Lord is mighty" (Joshua 4:24 ESV). David commanded us to "sing to the Lord, *all the earth*! . . . Declare his glory among the nations, his marvelous works among *all the peoples*!" (Psalm 96:1, 3 ESV). God spoke to us through Isaiah: "I will make you as a light for the nations, that my salvation may reach to the *end of the earth*" (Isaiah 49:6 ESV). His vision for the end of history includes "people for God from *every* tribe, language, people, and nation" (Revelation 5:9 NCV).

God longs to proclaim his greatness in all 6,909 languages that exist in the world today.[20] He loves subcultures: the gypsies of Turkey, the hippies of California, the cowboys and rednecks of West Texas. He has a heart for bikers and hikers, tree huggers and academics. Single moms. Gray-flanneled executives. He loves all people groups and equips us to be his voice. He commissions common Galileans, Nebraskans, Brazilians, and Koreans to speak the languages of the peoples of the world. He teaches us the vocabulary of distant lands, the dialect of the discouraged neighbor, the vernacular of the lonely heart, and the idiom of the young student. God outfits his followers to cross cultures and touch hearts.

–OUTLIVE YOUR LIFE

Lord God, you love the entire world. You want your kingdom to include people from every corner of this earth. You care about the needs of all people groups, and you want us to touch them with your love. Cleanse our hearts from any thoughts of superiority or inferiority among the people of the world. Let us embrace all tribes and nations and cultures and speak to them the language of your love. Teach us to be gracious in our speech and to bring out the best in others. We want to cross cultures and touch hearts, amen.

I will also give You as a light to the Gentiles, that
You should be My salvation to the ends of the earth.

ISAIAH 49:6

*Use your whole body as an instrument
to do what is right for the glory of God.*

Romans 6:13 nlt

God's Tool, God's Temple

When it comes to our bodies, the Bible declares that we don't own them. "You are no longer your own. God paid a great price for you. So use your body to honor God" (1 Corinthians 6:19–20 cev).

Use your body to indulge your passions? To grab attention? To express your opinions? No. Use your body to honor God. "Use your whole body as an instrument to do what is right for the glory of God" (Romans 6:13 nlt). Your body is God's instrument, intended for his work and for his glory. . . .

What work is more important than God's? Doesn't it stand to reason that God's tools should be maintained? . . .

Maintain God's instrument. Feed it. Rest it. When he needs a sturdy implement—a servant who is rested enough to serve, fueled enough to work, alert enough to think—let him find one in you. He uses you. . . .

Your body, God's tool. Maintain it.

Your body, God's temple. Respect it.

"God owns the whole works. So let people see God in and through your body" (1 Corinthians 6:20 msg).

Manage God's house in such a way that passersby stop and notice. "Who lives in that house?" they will ask. And when they hear the answer, God will be honored.

–It's Not About Me

Heavenly Father, our bodies belong to you; they do not belong to us. We are your children, and we want to use our bodies as tools to honor you. Help us to be faithful to care for our bodies with proper food and rest and exercise. Teach us how to be good stewards of the bodies you created for us. Forgive us when we do not take care of what really belongs to you. May we be faithful to maintain and respect our bodies in a way that brings honor and glory to you, amen.

Do you not know that your body is the temple of the Holy Spirit who is in you, whom you have from God, and you are not your own?

1 Corinthians 6:19

To be carnally minded is death, but to be spiritually minded is life and peace.

Romans 8:6

For all have sinned and fall short of the glory of God.

ROMANS 3:23

FORGIVEN TO FORGIVE

Who wants to live with yesterday's rubble? Who wants to hoard the trash of the past? You don't, do you?

Or do you?

Not in your house, mind you, but in your heart? Not the junk of papers and boxes, but the remnants of anger and hurt. Do you pack-rat pain? Amass offenses? Record slights?

A tour of your heart might be telling. A pile of rejections stockpiled in one corner. Accumulated insults filling another. Images of unkind people lining the wall, littering the floor.

No one can blame you. Innocence takers, promise breakers, wound makers—you've had your share. Yet doesn't it make sense to get rid of their trash? Jesus says: *Give the grace you've been given.*

Let's calculate our indebtedness to him. How often do you sin, hmm, in an hour? To sin is to "fall short" (Romans 3:23). Worry is falling short on faith. Impatience is falling short on kindness. The critical spirit falls short on love. How often do you come up short with God? For the sake of discussion, let's say ten times an hour and tally the results. Ten sins an hour, times sixteen waking hours (assuming we don't sin in our sleep), times 365 days a year, times the average male life span of seventy-four years. I'm rounding the total off at 4,300,000 sins per person.

Tell me, how do you plan to pay God for your 4.3 million sin increments? Your payout is unachievable. Unreachable. You're swimming in a Pacific Ocean of debt.

Yet God pardons the zillion sins of selfish humanity. Forgives 60 million sin-filled days. "Out of sheer generosity he put us in right standing with himself. A pure gift. . . ." (Romans 3:24 MSG).

Multimillion-dollar forgiveness should produce a multimillion-dollar forgiver, shouldn't it?

—*Every Day Deserves a Chance*

Gracious Father, you have forgiven selfish humanity for every selfish sin. You have reached out in grace, mercy, and forgiveness without keeping count. When we are tempted to withhold forgiveness from others, may we remember how often you have forgiven us. Teach us to be as generous to others as you have been to us. May we never tire of being compassionate forgivers, amen.

Forgive us our debts, as we forgive our debtors.

MATTHEW 6:12

Do not provoke your children to wrath, but bring them up
in the training and admonition of the Lord.

EPHESIANS 6:4

CHERISH YOUR CHILDREN

Quiet heroes dot the landscape of our society. They don't wear ribbons or kiss trophics; they wear spit-up and kiss boo-boos. They don't make the headlines, but they do sew the hemlines and check the outlines and stand on the sidelines. You won't find their names on the Nobel Prize short list, but you will find their names on the home-room, carpool, and Bible teacher lists.

They are parents, both by blood and deed, name and calendar. Heroes. News programs don't call them. But that's okay. Because their kids do . . . They call them Mom. They call them Dad. And these moms and dads, more valuable than all the executives and lawmakers west of the Mississippi, quietly hold the world together.

Be numbered among them. Read books to your kids. Play ball while you can and they want you to. Make it your aim to watch every game they play, read every story they write, hear every recital in which they perform.

Children spell love with four letters: T-I-M-E. Not just quality time, but hang time, downtime, anytime, all the time. Your children are not your hobby; they are your calling.

Cherish the children who share your name.

—FACING YOUR GIANTS

Lord God, when you give us children, you give us a precious treasure. May we be serious about raising our children to serve you. Teach us how to train them to love you and serve you. May we be good examples to them of godliness. May our lives reflect your character. May our mouths speak forth your words. May our hearts be filled with compassion and wisdom to help our children fulfill your purpose for their lives, amen.

"See that you do not look down on one of these little ones. For I tell you that their angels in heaven always see the face of my Father in heaven."

MATTHEW 18:10 NIV

"Whoever welcomes one of these little children in my name welcomes me; and whoever welcomes me does not welcome me but the one who sent me."

MARK 9:37 NIV

Walk in love, as Christ also has loved us and given Himself for us. . . .

EPHESIANS 5:2

PEOPLE OF HOSPITALITY

Is it just me, or is human contact going the way of the snow leopard? There was a time when every activity spurred a conversation. Service your car; greet the attendant. Deposit a check at the bank; chat with the teller about the weather. Buy a gift, and speak with the sales-clerk. Not now. You can gas up with a credit card, make deposits online, and order a gift over the Internet. You can cycle through a day of business and never say *hello*.

Call us a fast society, an efficient society, but don't call us a personal society. Our society is set up for isola-tion. We wear earbuds when we exercise. We communicate via e-mail and text messages. We enter and exit our houses with gates and garage door openers. Our mantra: "I leave you alone. You leave me alone."

Yet God wants his people to be an exception. Let everyone else go the way of computers and keyboards. God's children will be people of hospitality.

Long before the church had pulpits and baptister-ies, she had kitchens and dinner tables. "The believers met together in the Temple every day. They ate together *in their homes*, happy to share their food with joyful hearts" (Acts 2:46 NCV).

It's no wonder that the elders were to be "given to hospitality" (1 Timothy 3:2 KJV). The primary gathering place of the church was the home. . . .

Not everyone can serve in a foreign land, lead a relief effort, or volunteer at the downtown soup kitchen. But who can't be hospitable? Do you have a front door? A table? Chairs? Bread and meat for sandwiches?

Congratulations! You just qualified to serve in the most ancient of ministries: hospitality.

–OUTLIVE YOUR LIFE

Lord Jesus, may we open our homes to serve others. May we give a meal or a minute or a meaningful time of fellowship to others. May we joyfully share what we can in your name to bring hope and healing to the hurting, amen.

Every day they continued to meet together in the temple courts. They broke bread in their homes and ate together with glad and sincere hearts, . . .

ACTS 2:46 NIV

Lord, I believe; help my unbelief!

MARK 9:24

A PARENT'S CONCERNS

Jairus was a Capernaum community leader, "one of the rulers of the synagogue" (Mark 5:22). Mayor, bishop, and ombudsman, all in one. The kind of man a city would send to welcome a celebrity. But when Jairus approached Jesus on the Galilean shoreline, he wasn't representing his village; he was pleading on behalf of his child.

Urgency stripped the formalities from his greeting. He issued no salutation or compliment, just a prayer of panic. The gospel reads: "[Jairus] fell at his feet, pleading fervently with him. 'My little daughter is dying,' he said. 'Please come and lay your hands on her; heal her so she can live'" (vv. 22–23 NLT).

Jairus isn't the only parent to run onto gospel pages on behalf of a child. A mother stormed out of the Canaanite hills, crying, "Mercy, Master, Son of David! My daughter is cruelly afflicted by an evil spirit" (Matthew 15:22 MSG). A father of a seizure-tormented boy sought help from the disciples, then Jesus. He cried out with tears, "Lord, I believe; help my unbelief!" (Mark 9:24).

The Canaanite mother. The father of the epileptic boy. Jairus. These three parents form an unwitting New

Testament society: struggling parents of stricken children. They held the end of their rope in one hand and reached toward Christ with the other. In each case Jesus responded. He never turned one away.

His consistent kindness issues a welcome announcement: Jesus heeds the concern in the parent's heart.

—*FEARLESS*

Loving Father, every day brings opportunities for parents to panic about their children. There are so many unknown dangers and potential pitfalls we cannot control. But you are in control, Father. So we plead on behalf of our children. We ask you to protect them, to guide them, and to give us wisdom to raise them for your glory and honor. We thank you that you care about the concerns of a parent's heart, amen.

One day some parents brought their children to Jesus
so he could lay his hands on them and pray for them.

MATTHEW 19:13 NLT

> *"You shall receive power when the Holy Spirit has come upon you; and you shall be witnesses to Me in Jerusalem, and in all Judea and Samaria, and to the end of the earth."*
>
> ACTS 1:8

"YOU WILL BE MY WITNESSES"

The tall one in the corner—that's Peter. Galilee thickened his accent. Fishing nets thickened his hands. Stubbornness thickened his skull. His biggest catch in life thus far has come with fins and gills. Odd. The guy pegged to lead the next great work of God knows more about bass and boat docks than he does about Roman culture or Egyptian leaders.

And his cronies: Andrew, James, Nathanael. Never traveled farther than a week's walk from home. Haven't studied the ways of Asia or the culture of Greece. Their passports aren't worn; their ways aren't sophisticated. Do they have any formal education?

In fact, what do they have? Humility? They jockeyed for cabinet positions. Sound theology? Peter told Jesus to forget the cross. Sensitivity? John wanted to torch the Gentiles. Loyalty? When Jesus needed prayers, they snoozed. When Jesus was arrested, they ran. Thanks to their cowardice, Christ had more enemies than friends at his execution.

Yet look at them six weeks later, crammed into the

second floor of a Jerusalem house, abuzz as if they'd just won tickets to the World Cup Finals. High fives and wide eyes. Wondering what in the world Jesus had in mind with his final commission: "You will be my witnesses in Jerusalem, and in all Judea and Samaria, and to the ends of the earth" (Acts 1:8 NIV).

You hillbillies will be my witnesses.

You uneducated and simple folk will be my witnesses.

You who once called me crazy, who shouted at me in the boat and doubted me in the Upper Room.

You will be my witnesses.

You will spearhead a movement that will explode out of Jerusalem like a just-opened fire hydrant and spill into the ends of the earth: into the streets of Paris, the districts of Rome, and the ports of Athens, Istanbul, Shanghai, and Buenos Aires.

–OUTLIVE YOUR LIFE

Lord Jesus, you are the centerpiece of life for us. Without you we would be nothing. Before you left earth, you charged your disciples to tell others the good news of salvation. Guide us now as we live our lives to be witnesses for you. Make us bold to proclaim the good tidings, amen.

<hr>

Fight the good fight of faith . . . to which you were also called and have confessed the good confession in the presence of many witnesses.

1 TIMOTHY 6:12

MAKE GOD KNOWN

As heaven's advertising agency, we promote God in every area of life, including success.

That's right—even your success is intended to reflect God. Listen to the reminder Moses gave the children of Israel: "Remember He is the one the LORD your God who gives you power to be successful, in order to fulfill the covenant he made with your ancestors" (Deuteronomy 8:18 NLT).

From where does success come? God. "It is the LORD your God who gives you power to become successful."

And why does he give it? For his reputation. "To fulfill the covenant he made with your ancestors."

God blessed Israel in order to billboard his faithfulness. When foreigners saw the fruitful farms of the Promised Land, God did not want them to think about the farmer but the farmer's Maker. Their success advertised God.

Nothing has changed. God lets you excel so you can make him known. And you can be sure of one thing: God will make you good at something. This is his principle: "True humility and fear of the LORD lead to riches, honor, and long life" (Proverbs 22:4 NLT). . . .

"We are ambassadors for Christ, as though God were making an appeal through us" (2 Corinthians 5:20 NASB). The ambassador has a singular aim—to represent his king. He promotes the king's agenda, protects the king's reputation, and presents the king's will. The ambassador elevates the name of the king.

May we do the same. May God rescue us from self-centered thinking. May we have no higher goal than to see someone think more highly of our Father, our King.

–*It's Not About Me*

Father, enable us to serve you with our whole hearts. Show us how to love, serve, help, teach, and care. May your will be done here on earth and in our lives. Teach us to center our goals and plans and ambitions on you. May the world know what an amazing and loving Savior you are, amen.

"He who believes in Me, the works that I do he will do also;
and greater works than these he will do."

John 14:12

"Blessed are the merciful, for they shall obtain mercy."

MATTHEW 5:7

WE CHOOSE TO GIVE GRACE

Forgiveness is, at its core, choosing to see your offender with different eyes. When some Moravian missionaries took the message of God to the Eskimos, the missionaries struggled to find a word in the native language for forgiveness. They finally landed on this cumbersome twenty-four-letter choice: *issumagijoujungnainermik.* This formidable assembly of letters is literally translated "not being able to think about it anymore."[21]

To forgive is to move on, not to think about the offense anymore. You don't excuse him, endorse her, or embrace them. You just route thoughts about them through heaven. You see your enemy as God's child and revenge as God's job.

By the way, how can we grace-recipients do anything less? Dare we ask God for grace when we refuse to give it? This is a huge issue in Scripture. Jesus was tough on sinners who refused to forgive other sinners. Remember his story about the servant freshly forgiven a debt of millions who refused to forgive a debt equal to a few dollars? He stirred the wrath of God: "You evil servant! I forgave you that tremendous debt. . . . Shouldn't you have mercy . . . just as I had mercy on you?" (Matthew 18:32–33 NLT).

In the final sum, we give grace because we've been given grace.

—*FACING YOUR GIANTS*

O Lord, Thank you for forgiving every sin of everyone who calls you Lord. May we be as merciful to others as you have been to your children. Teach us not only to forgive but also to forget about the offense. Fill our hearts with a willingness to leave the consequences in your hands. As you forgave a debt we could never pay, so we choose to forgive the debts of others, amen.

Forgive as the Lord forgave you.

COLOSSIANS 3:13 NIV

In Him we have redemption through His blood, the forgiveness of sins, according to the riches of His grace. . . .

EPHESIANS 1:7

He who heeds the word wisely will find good,
and whoever trusts in the LORD, happy is he.

GOD'S GIFT TO MARRIAGE

"Don't you realize that your body is the temple of the Holy Spirit, who lives in you?" (1 Corinthians 6:19 NLT). Paul wrote these words to counter the Corinthian sex obsession. "Run away from sexual sin!" reads the prior sentence. "No other sin so clearly affects the body as this one does. For sexual immorality is a sin against your own body" (v. 18 NLT).

What a salmon scripture! No message swims more upstream than this one. You know the sexual anthem of our day: "I'll do what I want. It's my body." God's firm response? "No, it's not. It's mine."

Be quick to understand, God is not antisex. Dismiss any notion that God is antiaffection and antiintercourse. After all, he developed the whole package. Sex was his idea. From his perspective, sex is nothing short of holy.

He views sexual intimacy the way I view our family Bible. Passed down from my father's side, the volume is one hundred years old and twelve inches thick. Replete with lithographs, scribblings, and a family tree, it is, in my estimation, beyond value. Hence, I use it carefully.

When I need a step stool, I don't reach for the Bible.

If the foot of my bed breaks, I don't use the family Bible as a prop. When we need old paper for wrapping, we don't rip a sheet out of this book. We reserve the heirloom for special times and keep it in a chosen place.

Regard sex the same way—as a holy gift to be opened in a special place at special times. The special place is marriage, and the time is with your spouse.

—IT'S NOT ABOUT ME

Lord God, may we treat the marriage covenant as sacred. May we resist any temptation to break down the walls of protection around our marriage. We want to honor you with our bodies and our sacred vows, amen.

Sexual immorality is a sin against your own body.

1 CORINTHIANS 6:18 NLT

You must abstain from . . . sexual immorality.
If you do this, you will do well.

ACTS 15:29 NLT

LABEL THEM OR LOVE THEM?

Categorizing others creates distance and gives us a convenient exit strategy for avoiding involvement.

Jesus took an entirely different approach. He was all about including people, not excluding them. "The Word became flesh and blood, and moved into the neighborhood" (John 1:14 MSG). Jesus touched lepers and loved foreigners and spent so much time with partygoers that people called him a "lush, a friend of the riffraff" (Matthew 11:19 MSG). Racism couldn't keep him from the Samaritan woman; demons couldn't keep him from the demoniac. His Facebook page included the likes of Zacchaeus the Ponzi-meister, Matthew the IRS agent, and some floozy he met at Simon's house. Jesus spent thirty-three years walking in the mess of this world. "He had equal status with God but didn't think so much of himself that he had to cling to the advantages of that status no matter what. Not at all. When the time came, he set aside the privileges of deity and took on the status of a slave, became *human*!" (Philippians 2:6–7 MSG). . . .

God calls us to change the way we look at people. Not to see them as Gentiles or Jews, insiders or outsiders, liberals or conservatives. Not to label. To label is to libel. "We have stopped evaluating others from a human point of view" (2 Corinthians 5:16 NLT).

Let's view people differently; let's view them as we do ourselves. Blemished, perhaps. Unfinished, for certain.

In our lifetimes you and I are going to come across some discarded people. Tossed out. Sometimes tossed out by a church. And we get to choose. Neglect or rescue? Label them or love them? We know Jesus' choice. Just look at what he did with us.

—OUTLIVE YOUR LIFE

Precious Savior, change the way we look at people. Forgive us for categorizing and classifying others. We have failed you by labeling people and keeping them at a distance. When you walked here on earth you reached out to all people, even the lepers and sinners. You came near to outcasts and misfits, and you touched them with love. Teach us to walk in the mess of the world like you did, breaking down barriers and reaching out with a helping hand, amen.

As we have opportunity, let us do good to all.

GALATIANS 6:10

May the God of peace . . . make you complete
in every good work to do His will. . . .
HEBREWS 13:20–21

KINDNESS WITHOUT COMPENSATION

Want to snatch a day from the manacles of boredom? Do overgenerous deeds, acts beyond reimbursement. Kindness without compensation. Do a deed for which you cannot be repaid.

Here's another idea. *Get over yourself.*

Moses did. One of history's foremost leaders was "a very humble man, more humble than anyone else on the face of the earth" (Numbers 12:3 NIV).

Mary did. When Jesus called her womb his home, she did not boast; she simply confessed: "I'm the Lord's maid, ready to serve" (Luke 1:38 MSG).

John the Baptist did. Though a blood relative of God on earth, he made this choice: "This is the assigned moment for him to move into the center, while I slip off to the sidelines" (John 3:30 MSG).

Most of all, Jesus did. "Jesus . . . was given a position 'a little lower than the angels'" (Hebrews 2:9 NLT).

Jesus chose the servants' quarters. Can't we?

We're important, but not essential; valuable, but not indispensable. We have a part in the play, but we are not the main act. A song to sing, but we are not the featured voice. God is.

He did well before our birth; he'll do fine after our deaths. He started it all, sustains it all, and will bring it all to a glorious climax. In the meantime, we have this high privilege: to surrender personal goals, discover the thrill of the doubled distance, do deeds for which we cannot be paid, seek problems that others avoid, deny ourselves, take up our crosses, and follow Christ.

—*Every Day Deserves a Chance*

Lord and Savior, you gave up your throne in heaven to be born as a tiny baby. You grew up the son of a humble carpenter. As a man here on earth, you chose the servants' quarters. When we start thinking we are indispensable, remind us, Lord, that we are important but not essential. You are the main act. Thank you for letting us have even a small part to play in your grand scheme of things. May we be willing to go the extra mile and to deny ourselves for the sake of your kingdom, amen.

Let nothing be done through selfish ambition or conceit, but in lowliness of mind let each esteem others better than himself.

PHILIPPIANS 2:3

God made all things, and everything continues through him and for him. To him be the glory forever.

OUR PURPOSE

If we boast at all, we "boast in the Lord" (2 Corinthians 10:17 NASB).

The breath you took as you read that last sentence was given to you for one reason, that you might for another moment "reflect the Lord's glory" (3:18 NIV). God awoke you and me this morning for one purpose: "Declare his glory among the nations, his marvelous deeds among all peoples" (1 Chronicles 16:24 NIV).

"God made all things, and everything continues through him and *for* him. To him be the glory forever" (Romans 11:36 NCV). "There is only one God, the Father, who created everything, and *we exist for him*" (1 Corinthians 8:6 NLT).

Why does the earth spin? For him.

Why do you have talents and abilities? For him.

Why do you have money or poverty? For him.

Strength or struggles? For him.

Everything and everyone exists to reveal his glory.

Including you.

–IT'S NOT ABOUT ME

Father in heaven, may our only boast be in you. You have created everything and we exist for you. The earth spins for you. The moon shines for you. The flowers burst into bloom for you. May our lives bring glory to you. Use our talents and abilities for you. All our strengths and struggles are for you. Our hearts sing only for you and give you glory. May that always be the purpose and passion of our lives, amen.

Sing to Him, sing psalms to Him; talk of all His wondrous works!

1 CHRONICLES 16:9

I thought it good to declare the signs and wonders
that the Most High God has worked for me.

DANIEL 4:2

O, that men would give thanks to the LORD for this goodness.

PSALM 107:8

The soul of Jonathan was knit to the soul of David,
and Jonathan loved him as his own soul.

1 SAMUEL 18:1

YOU HAVE A FRIEND IN JESUS

Jonathan could have been as jealous of David as Saul. As Saul's son, he stood to inherit the throne. A noble soldier himself, he was fighting Philistines while David was still feeding sheep.

Jonathan had reason to despise David, but he didn't. He was gracious. Gracious because the hand of the Master Weaver took his and David's hearts and stitched a seam between them. "The soul of Jonathan was knit to the soul of David, and Jonathan loved him as his own soul" (1 Samuel 18:1).

As if the two hearts were two fabrics, God "needle and threaded" them together. So interwoven that when one moved, the other felt it. When one was stretched, the other knew it. . . .

Oh, to have a friend like Jonathan. A soul mate who protects you, who seeks nothing but your interests, wants nothing but your happiness. An ally who lets you be you. You feel safe with that person. . . . God gave David such a friend.

He gave you one as well. David found a companion in a prince of Israel; you can find a friend in the King of

Israel, Jesus Christ. Has he not made a covenant with you? Among his final words were these: "I am with you always, even to the end of the age" (Matthew 28:20).

Has he not clothed you? He offers you "white garments, that you may be clothed, that the shame of your nakedness may not be revealed" (Revelation 3:18). Christ cloaks you with clothing suitable for heaven. . . .

Catalog his kindnesses. Everything from sunsets to salvation—look at what you have. . . . Let Jesus be the friend you need.

—*Facing Your Giants*

Precious Savior, you are the friend we need. We can trust you with our destiny. We find our identity in the life you plan out for us. We come to you freely in faith and love. In you we find help and hope for our daily needs. You are a friend who walks with us each minute and each step of the way. There is nowhere we can go that you haven't already been. Thank you for being our dearest friend, amen.

"Greater love has no one than this, than to lay down
one's life for his friends."

John 15:13

"Lo, I am with you always, even to the end of the age."

Matthew 28:20

Take in with all Christians the extravagant dimensions of Christ's love.
EPHESIANS 3:18 MSG

LOVED WITH A HEAVENLY LOVE

Your goodness can't win God's love. Nor can your badness lose it. But you can resist it.

I have a feeling that most people who defy and deny God do so more out of fear than conviction. For all our chest pumping and braggadocio, we are anxious folk—can't see a step into the future, can't hear the one who owns us. No wonder we try to gum the hand that feeds us.

But God reaches and touches. He speaks through the immensity of the Russian plain and the density of the Amazon rain forest. Through a physician's touch in Africa, a bowl of rice in India. Through a Japanese bow or a South American *abraço*. He's even been known to touch people through paragraphs like the ones you are reading. If he is touching you, let him.

Mark it down: God loves you with an unearthly love. You can't win it by being winsome. You can't lose it by being a loser. But you can be blind enough to resist it.

Don't. For heaven's sake, don't. For your sake, don't.

"Take in with all Christians the extravagant dimensions of Christ's love. Reach out and experience the breadth! Test its length! Plumb the depths! Rise to the heights! Live full lives, full in the fullness of God" (Ephesians 3:18–19 MSG). Others demote you. God claims you. Let the definitive voice of the universe say, "You're still a part of my plan." . . .

God will not let you go. He has handcuffed himself to you in love. And he owns the only key. You need not win his love. You already have it. And since you can't win it, you can't lose it.

—3:16: THE NUMBERS OF HOPE

Lord, you have reminded us of your loving plan of salvation. May we never try to replace your sacrificial gift with our own attempts to be good enough to deserve it. May we never forget that we don't have to win your love. May we never fear that we might lose your love. Make us bold to tell others of this amazing gift, amen.

❧

As the mountains surround Jerusalem,
so the LORD surrounds His people.

PSALM 125:2

May you experience the love of Christ,
though it is too great to understand fully.

EPHESIANS 3:19 NLT

"He who has My commandments and keeps them, it is he who loves Me. And he who loves Me will be loved by My Father."

REFLECTING THE LOVE OF GOD

We are God's mirrors.

"And we, with our unveiled faces reflecting like mirrors the brightness of the Lord, all grow brighter and brighter as we are turned into the image that we reflect; this is the work of the Lord who is Spirit" (2 Corinthians 3:18 JB).

Paul paralleled the Christian experience to the Mount Sinai experience of Moses. After the patriarch *beheld* the glory of God, his face *reflected* the glory of God. "The people of Israel could not bear to look at Moses' face. For his face shone with the glory of God" (2 Corinthians 3:7 NLT). . . .

Upon beholding God, Moses could not help but reflect God. *The brightness he saw was the brightness he became.* Beholding led to becoming. Becoming led to reflecting. . . .

What does it mean to behold your face in a mirror? A quick glance? A casual look? No. To behold is to study, to stare, to contemplate. Beholding God's glory, then, is no side look or occasional glance; this beholding is a serious pondering.

Isn't that what we have done? We have camped at the foot of Mount Sinai and beheld the glory of God. Wisdom unsearchable. Purity unspotted. Years unending. Strength undaunted. Love immeasurable. Glimpses of the glory of God.

As we behold his glory, dare we pray that we, like Moses, will reflect it? Dare we hope to be mirrors in the hands of God, the reflection of the light of God?

This is the call.

–*It's Not About Me*

Father God, your wisdom is unsearchable. Your purity unspotted. Your years are unending and your strength is undaunted. Your grace and love are immeasurable. You are a glorious God, full of compassion and kindness. When we reflect on you, our hearts expand with praise and thanksgiving. Your mercy is the wonder of the world. You make us strong and you give us peace. We want our lives to reflect the light of your majesty, amen.

The Son reflects the glory of God and shows exactly what He is like.

HEBREWS 1:3 NCV

So all of us who have had that veil removed can
see and reflect the glory of the Lord.

2 CORINTHIANS 3:18 NLT

I have made myself a servant to all, that I might win the more.

1 CORINTHIANS 9:19

"FOLLOW ME"

Does Christ still use simple folks like us to change the world?

Edith would say yes.

Edith Hayes was a spry eighty-year-old with thinning white hair, a wiry five-foot frame, and an unquenchable compassion for South Florida's cancer patients. I was fresh out of seminary in 1979 and sitting in an office of unpacked books when she walked in and introduced herself: "My name is Edith, and I help cancer patients." She extended her hand. I offered a chair. She politely declined. "Too busy. You'll see my team here at the church building every Tuesday morning. You're welcome to come, but if you come, we'll put you to work." . . .

Edith rented an alley apartment, lived on her late husband's pension, wore glasses that magnified her pupils, and ducked applause like artillery fire.

God doesn't call the qualified. He qualifies the called. Don't let Satan convince you otherwise. He will try. He will tell you that God has an IQ requirement or an entry fee. That he employs only specialists and experts, governments and high-powered personalities. When Satan whispers such lies, dismiss him with this truth: God stampeded the first-century society with swaybacks, not thoroughbreds. Before Jesus came along, the disciples were loading trucks, coaching soccer, and selling Slurpee drinks at the convenience store. Their collars were blue, and their hands were calloused, and there is no evidence that Jesus chose them because they were smarter or nicer than the guy next door. The one thing they had going for them was a willingness to take a step when Jesus said, "Follow me."

Are you more dinghy than cruise ship? More stand-in than movie star? More plumber than executive? More blue jeans than blue blood? Congratulations. God changes the world with folks like you.

–Outlive Your Life

Lord Jesus, thank you for not calling the qualified but qualifying those you call. You don't require us to be a specialist or an expert to be used by you. You simply choose those who will follow you. You don't stipulate diplomas or dollars or dignity. You simply ask for dedication. You choose to change the world through simple folks like me who are willing to say yes. Thank you, amen.

Now all the glory to God, who is able, through his mighty power at work within us, to accomplish infinitely more than we might ask or think.

EPHESIANS 3:20 NLT

"The work God wants you to do is this: Believe the One he sent."

ONE PATH LEADS TO GOD

Some historians clump Christ with Moses, Muhammad, Confucius, and other spiritual leaders. But Jesus refuses to share the page. He declares, "I am the way, and the truth, and the life; no one comes to the Father, but by me" (John 14:6 RSV). He could have scored more points in political correctness had he said, "I know the way," or, "I show the way." Yet he speaks not of what he does but of who he is: *I am the way.*

His followers refused to soften or shift the spotlight. Peter announced: "There is salvation in no one else! God has given no other name under heaven by which we must be saved" (Acts 4:12 NLT).

Many recoil at such definitiveness. John 14:6 and Acts 4:12 sound primitive in this era of broadbands and broad minds. The world is shrinking, cultures are blending, borders are bending; this is the day of inclusion. All roads lead to heaven, right?

But can they? The sentence makes good talk show fodder, but is it accurate? Can all approaches to God be correct?

How can all religions lead to God when they are so different? We don't tolerate such illogic in other matters.

We don't pretend that all roads lead to London or all ships sail to Australia. All flights don't land in Rome. . . .

Every path does not lead to God. Jesus blazed a stand-alone trail void of self-salvation. He cleared a one-of-a-kind passageway uncluttered by human effort. Christ came, not for the strong, but for the weak; not for the righteous, but for the sinner. We enter his way upon confession of our need, not completion of our deeds. He offers a unique-to-him invitation in which he works and we trust, he dies and we live, he invites and we believe.

We believe in him.

–3:46: The Numbers of Hope

Gracious Father, you are not willing that any person spend life without you. You have made a pathway of salvation for all who choose to walk on that way. The Bible teaches us that your Son, Jesus, is the way and the truth. There are not many ways to make our hearts right before you. There is only one way, and that is through the death of Jesus Christ. Thank you that you offer this unique invitation of salvation to all who choose to believe in you, amen.

Nor is there salvation in any other; for there is no other name under heaven given among men by which we must be saved.

Acts 4:12

Behold, children are a heritage from the LORD,
the fruit of the womb is a reward.

PSALM 127:3

OUR KIDS ARE GOD'S KIDS

The semitruck of parenting comes loaded with fears. We fear failing the child, forgetting the child. Will we have enough money? Enough answers? Enough diapers? Enough drawer space? Vaccinations. Educations. Homework. Homecoming. It's enough to keep a parent awake at night. . . .

Fear distilleries concoct a high-octane brew for parents—a primal, gut-wrenching, pulse-stilling dose. Whether Mom and Dad keep vigil outside a neonatal unit, make weekly visits to a juvenile prison, or hear the crunch of a bike and the cry of a child in the driveway, their reaction is the same: "I have to do something." No parent can sit still while his or her child suffers. . . .

But our kids were God's kids first. "Don't you see that children are God's best gift? the fruit of the womb his generous legacy?" (Psalm 127:3 MSG). Before they were ours, they were his. Even as they are ours, they are still his.

We tend to forget this fact, regarding our children as "our" children, as though we have the final say in their health and welfare. We don't. All people are God's people, including the small people who sit at our tables. Wise are the parents who regularly give their children back to God.

—FEARLESS

Heavenly Father, you surely know the concerns and burdens of a parent's heart. You are a father yourself. When we feel overwhelmed with the responsibilities of raising our children, may we remember that they are your children first. You created them and gave them as a gift to us. May we daily give them back to you and rest calmly in your promise to give us wisdom and guidance to raise them for you, amen.

He will turn the hearts of the fathers to their children,
and the hearts of the children to their fathers.

MALACHI 4:6 NIV

Train a child in the way he should go,
and when he is old he will not turn from it.

PROVERBS 22:6 NIV

*Holy, holy, holy is the L*ORD *of hosts.*

LOVED BY THE ETERNAL GOD

"To whom, then, will you compare God?" the prophet invites (Isaiah 40:18 NIV). To whom indeed? "Human hands can't serve his needs—for he has no needs" (Acts 17:25 NLT). You and I start our days needy. Indeed, basic needs prompt us to climb out of bed. Not God. Uncreated and self-sustaining, he depends on nothing and no one. Never taken a nap or a breath. Needs no food, counsel, or physician. "The Father has life in himself" (John 5:26 NIV). Life is to God what wetness is to water and air is to wind. He is not just alive but life itself. . . .

Hence, he always is. "Before the mountains were brought forth, or ever You had formed the earth and the world, even from everlasting to everlasting, You are God" (Psalm 90:2).

God never began and will never cease. He exists endlessly, always. "The number of His years is unsearchable" (Job 36:26 NASB).

Even so, let's try to search them. Let every speck of sand, from the Sahara to South Beach, represent a billion years of God's existence. With some super vacuum, suck and then blow all the particles into a mountain, and count how many you have. Multiply your total by a billion and listen as God reminds: "They don't repre-sent a fraction of my existence."

He is "the eternal God" (Romans 16:26 NIV). . . . He was something before anything else was. When the first angel lifted the first wing, God had already always been.

Most staggering of all, he has never messed up. Not once. . . . God is holy. Every decision, exact. Each word, appropriate. Never out-of-bounds or out of place. Not even tempted to make a mistake. . . . No wonder he said, "I am God, and there is none like me" (Isaiah 46:9 NIV).

—3:16: THE NUMBERS OF HOPE

Gracious God, you are incomparable and you are eternal. You have always been and always will be. You are the crea-tor of life: physical life and spiritual life. You are holy and mighty beyond measure. Yet you love and care for each of your children. Your eternal presence gives hope and courage. We rely on you and trust you. You are good to your children, and you are committed to your children. Thank you and praise you, amen.

Before the mountains were brought forth, or ever You had formed the earth and the world, even from everlasting to everlasting, You are God.

PSALM 90:2

PERSONAL NOTES

PERSONAL NOTES

PERSONAL NOTES

PERSONAL NOTES

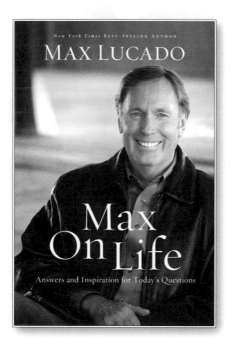

INSPIRATION TWICE A DAY, EVERY DAY!

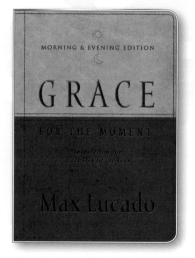

Grace for the Moment – Morning and Evening Edition
978-1-4041-1374-9, $19.99

Grace for the Moment continues to touch lives as it emphasizes the help and hope of God in everyday moments and offers enough inspiration to carry you through the busiest of days. Max Lucado, America's leading inspirational author, fills each day's reading with vivid words that offer guidelines for grace-filled living.

In this special edition, readers can sit quietly, including the full texts of Volumes I and II, and enjoy one reading in the morning in preparation for what lies ahead and one in the evening in reflection of what has gone by.

NOTES

1. Frederick Dale Bruner, *The Christbook: Matthew—A Commentary*, rev. and exp. ed. (Dallas: Word Publishing, 1987), 210.

2. C. J. Mahaney, "Loving the Church," audiotape of message at Covenant Life Church, Gaithersburg, MD, n.d., quoted in Randy Alcorn, *Heaven* (Wheaton, IL: Tyndale House, 2004), xxii.

3. John Haggai, *How to Win Over Worry: A Practical Formula for Successful Living* (Eugene, OR: Harvest House Publishers, 1987), 109.

4. Bob Russell, "Reinstated," *Favorite Stories from Bob Russell*, vol. 5, CD-ROM, Southeast Christian Church, Louisville, KY, 2005.

5. Fred Lowery, *Covenant Marriage: Staying Together for Life* (West Monroe, LA: Howard Publishing, 2002), 44.

6. Lowery, *Covenant Marriage*, 45.

7. Archibald Naismith, *2400 Outlines, Notes, Quotes, and Anecdotes for Sermons* (1967; repr., Grand Rapids: Baker Book House, 1991), #1063.

8. Rubel Shelly, *The ABCs of the Christian Faith* (Nashville, TN: Wineskins, 1998), 21–22.

9. Rick Atchley, "God's Love Does Not Change," audiocassette of a sermon, Richland Hills Church of Christ, Fort Worth, TX, 28 July 1996.

10. *1041 Sermon Illustrations, Ideas, and Expositions: Treasury of the Christian World*, ed. A. Gordon Nasby (1953; repr., Harper & Brothers, Ann Arbor, Michigan), 109.

11. *1041 Sermon Illustrations, Ideas, and Expositions: Treasury of the Christian World*, ed. A. Gordon Nasby (1953, Harper & Brothers, Ann Arbor, Michigan), 213.

12. Eugene H. Peterson, *Run with the Horses: The Quest for Life at Its Best* (Madison, WI: InterVarsity Press, 1983), 115.

13. Associated Press, "450 Sheep Jump to their Deaths in Turkey," 8 July 2005.

14. Andy Christofides, *The Life Sentence: John 3:16* (Waynesboro, GA: Paternoster Publishing, 2002), 11.

15. Guillermo Gonzalez and Jay W. Richards, *The Privileged Planet: How Our Place in the Cosmos Is Designed for Discovery* (Washington, DC: Regenery Publishing, 2004), 143.

16. Christofides, *The Life Sentence*, 13.

17. "Liftoff to Space Exploration," NASA, http://liftoff.msfc.nasa.gov/academy/universe_travel.html.

18. Gary L. Thomas, *Sacred Marriage: What If God Designed Marriage to Make Us Holy More Than to Make Us Happy?* (Grand Rapids: Zondervan, 2000), 46–47.

19. F. W. Boreham, *Life Verses: The Bible's Impact on Famous Lives, Vol. Two* (Grand Rapids: Kregel Publications, 1994), 114–155.

20. M. Paul Lewis, *Ethnologue: Languages of the World*, 16th ed. (Dallas: SIL International, 2009), www.ethnologue.com.

21. M. Norville Young with Mary Hollingsworth, *Living Lights, Shining Stars: Ten Secrets to Becoming the Light of the World* (West Monroe, LA: Howard Publishing, 1997), 39.

SOURCES

All of the material in this book was originally published in the following books by Max Lucado. All copyrights to the original works are held by the author, Max Lucado.

It's Not About Me. Nashville: Thomas Nelson, Inc., 2004.

Facing Your Giants. Nashville: Thomas Nelson, Inc., 2006.

3:16: Numbers of Hope. Nashville: Thomas Nelson, Inc., 2007.

Every Day Deserves a Chance. Nashville: Thomas Nelson, Inc., 2007.

Fearless. Nashville: Thomas Nelson, Inc., 2009.

Outlive Your Life. Nashville: Thomas Nelson, Inc., 2010.